SEPTOPUS
Trouble on the
High Cs

Jyotin Goel is a feature film and television writer and director based in Mumbai. He wrote and directed the animated children's film, *Bird Idol*, for Warner Bros.

Rajiv Eipe studied Fine Arts at Sir J.J. School of Art, Mumbai; and Animation Film Design at the National Institute of Design, Ahmedabad. He currently lives in Bangalore and spends his time doing animation and illustration projects.

SEPTOPUS

Trouble on the
High Cs

JYOTIN GOEL
Illustrated by RAJIV EIPE

RED TURTLE
RUPA

Published in Red Turtle by
Rupa Publications India Pvt. Ltd 2016
7/16, Ansari Road, Daryaganj
New Delhi 110002

Sales Centres:
Allahabad Bengaluru Chennai
Hyderabad Jaipur Kathmandu
Kolkata Mumbai

Copyright © Jyotin Goel 2016
Illustrations copyright © Rupa Publications India Pvt. Ltd 2016

All rights reserved.
No part of this publication may be reproduced, transmitted,
or stored in a retrieval system, in any form or by any means,
electronic, mechanical, photocopying, recording or otherwise,
without the prior permission of the publisher.

This is a work of fiction. Names, characters, places and incidents
are either the product of the author's imagination or are used
fictitiously and any resemblance to any actual person,
living or dead, events or locales is entirely coincidental.

ISBN: 978-81-291-4208-5

First impression 2016

10 9 8 7 6 5 4 3 2 1

The moral right of the author has been asserted.

This book is sold subject to the condition that it shall not,
by way of trade or otherwise, be lent, resold, hired out, or otherwise circulated,
without the publisher's prior consent, in any form of binding or cover
other than that in which it is published.

For Jaeh,
our rising new star

I

'Hee hee hee!'

'Save your breath!' Irrit hissed at Po.

'Irrit' and 'Po'? Are those real names? Yes, they are. As odd as they sound, they are perfectly normal names—normal for octopuses, that is. As octopuses have eight tentacles, all octopus names end in '8'; but since the '8' is common to all octopuses, they just leave it out when talking to each other. So 'Po' is actually 'Po8' and 'Irrit' is actually 'Irrit8'. Confusing? Not for octopuses, who are easily the cleverest creatures on earth.

Anyway, Po chuckled when he shouldn't have and Irrit hissed irritatedly at him. Po stopped sniggering, but he couldn't help shaking with silent giggles. This was because Irrit and he were inking fins, spines and tails on Delic8, Clarin8, Gyr8 and Pyr8. Of course, they weren't actually smearing real, live octopuses. What they were doing was using their octopus ink to deface a poster advertising the Oct-estra, Goa Sea World's most popular attraction. Irrit and Po were green with jealousy at the popularity of the Oct-estra stars, who just happened to be the parents and siblings of their sworn enemy, Rot!

'Why should the Oct-estra be made up from just one family?' Irrit had complained to Po.

'It's nepotism!' Po railed.

'That's just what it is!' Irrit agreed. 'Nept…nepos… it's what you said it is!'

And to make their feelings known, the disgruntled duo had decided to mess up the poster. Making sure no Sea World keeper was about, Irrit and Po had sneaked out of the pool. They had slithered up to the poster (placed at the entrance of a special chamber where the Oct-estra performed) and had gone to work, smearing and splattering. Soon the poster was a sea of octopus ink and Irrit and Po gloated over the ugly scrawls marring the faces of the talented quartet. Octopuses, however, can stay out of water for only a few minutes, which is why Irrit had advised Po to save his breath. Now they needed to get back into the water to breathe and they turned and scurried back. Reaching the edge of the pool, they were about to plunge in when…

'I wouldn't do that if I were you,' said a voice.

Irrit and Po jumped in fright! Spinning around, they looked about guiltily—and spotted what looked like a fat, green tub basking in the sun on the platform above the pool.

Tumboo.

The troublesome twosome grinned. It was only Tumboo. The turtle smiled back, raised a lazy flipper and pointed towards a corner of the pool. Still grinning, Irrit and Po looked in the direction indicated. From the depths of the water rose a dark, triangular fin. It sliced through the pool ominously, the water rippling in its wake.

'A sha…sha…shark!' croaked Irrit.

'…bark…lark…park…' stuttered Po, who had a tendency to rhyme uncontrollably whenever his three hearts thudded with fright.

'That's Orca,' said Tumboo, helpfully.

'O...Orca?' Irrit spluttered. 'Is...is that a shark or w...whale?'

'Whale-shark,' replied Tumboo. 'Calls himself "Orca" because he wants to be a real whale. He can't, of course, so he's always bad-tempered.'

The shark fin glided through the water. Two pairs of octopus eyes helplessly followed its course, glued to the terrifying triangle.

'...Orca...Majorca...Minorca...' Po rhymed, scared silly.

'Shut up, Po!' barked Irrit, snapping out of his trance.

He knew they were in real trouble. Tumboo could sit in the sun, lazily breathing air, but Irrit and Po needed to get into the water—and fast! Could they slither in without Orca noticing? Irrit edged forward, but instantly the frightening fin turned and headed towards his end of the pool.

'Yow!' yelped Irrit, hurriedly pulling back from the edge.

'Ow!' cried Po, as Irrit stumbled over his tentacles.

Off-balance, their tentacles entangled, the two octopuses grabbed at each other and twirled and tangoed to the very edge of the pool. For a moment, they teetered on the rim; another step and they would have plunged into the shark-infested water! But with a desperate thrashing of tentacles they managed to dance back, gasping with terror.

'Encore!' Tumboo cried, clapping her flippers in appreciation of the octopuses' spontaneous salsa. 'Encore!'

'"Anchor"?' Irrit panted. 'What's she shouting "anchor" for?'

'"Encore", you ignorant jug of jelly!' grinned Tumboo. 'It means "do it again"!'

Irrit and Po, however, were in no mood to 'do it again'. Their choreographic exertions had drained almost every last breath from their bodies. They *had* to get oxygen, but with a bad-tempered shark just inches away, plunging into the pool was a definite no-no. They panted and gasped like fish out of water, which, of course, is exactly what they were.

'Need help?' Tumboo enquired, politely.

'W...We don't need h...help from an overweight tub o...of lard!'

'...card...hard...bard...'

'Shut up, Po!'

'...woe...low...no...'

'Well, I did have a plan, but...' Tumboo started lumbering away. 'See you around...maybe!'

A plan!

Irrit was extremely wary of Rot and Tumboo's plans, but the situation was desperate.

'Hey!' Irrit gasped. 'We...we're listening...'

Septopus

Tumboo grinned and turned towards the panting pair. 'Glad you changed your mind!' She indicated the hovering shark. 'What you need to do is distract him.'

'And how do we d...do that?' Irrit wheezed, sarcastically.

'Simple,' smiled Tumboo. 'I jump in. He comes after me. You get in and escape through the pipe into the next pool.'

Irrit looked at the turtle. The plan could work. Orca couldn't bite through Tumboo's tough shell, but he'd waste time trying to do so, allowing Irrit and Po to make good their escape. It seemed perfect. But...

'What's th...the catch?' Irrit panted.

'...latch...match...snatch...'

'Now that you mention it,' Tumboo mused, 'there *is* one thing...'

'I knew it!' Irrit said, breathing hard. 'O...out with it!'

'Okay. You know Sea World is putting on a show? A week from now?'

'Yeah. S...so?'

Tumboo indicated the defaced poster. 'Rot and I can't match your artistic talent, but we've composed a tune for the show.'

'T...tune?' Irrit spluttered.

'Let me hum it for you,' Tumboo said brightly, and started warbling a sprightly melody.

Irrit gawped at the tuneful turtle, wondering if she'd been out in the sun too long. Tumboo hummed on, throwing her head back, drawing in a lungful of air and belting out a final, ear-splitting high C.

'Well, that's the tune,' she smiled. 'Great, isn't it? Now all we need are the lyrics!'

'L...lyrics?'

'Everyone knows you have a way with words, Po,' she smiled innocently. 'Can you help us? We've even come up with the first line, but we're kind of stuck. It goes like this: *We're Irrit and Po, two rotters...*'

'Rotters?!!' protested Po.

'Well, we're not poets like you,' Tumboo said soothingly. 'If you've got a better word...rogues... rascals...rats...go right ahead. We're not fussy!'

'Y...you think I'm g...going to help you i...insult us?!' Po asked, his poetic feelings outraged.

'You're not?' Tumboo said, looking disappointed. 'I guess it's all about poetic temperament. You can't force inspiration.' She waved brightly at the drained duo and waddled off. 'Be seeing you...maybe!'

'W...wait!' Irrit gasped. 'S...stop!'

Tumboo looked back questioningly.

'W...we'll do it!' Irrit rasped. 'W...won't we, Po?'

'B...but that tub of lard, she called us "r...rotters"! "Ro..."'

Irrit clapped a tentacle over Po's runaway mouth. 'And that's w...what we are!' Irrit panted. Sticking his face close to Po's ear-sac, Irrit hissed, 'You've got a minute to come up with the w...words, you bubble-brained balladeer, or we g...go into the pool with that!' He jabbed a tentacle in the direction of the horrific fin.

Po's eyes went round with terror. 'I...I'll do it!' he squeaked.

Tumboo turned. 'Now isn't that nice!' She settled herself comfortably.

Po wheezed and gasped, his mind blank.

'Come on, c...come on!' panted Irrit.

The terrifying fin closed in on the pool's edge. Fear concentrates a mind wonderfully, even a vacant mind like Po's, and suddenly he spouted:

We're Irrit and Po, two rotters,
Much dumber are we than we think,
We do nothing but muddy the waters,
Soiling every clear thing with ink!

CHORUS: *Ohhh! Soiling and smearing with ink!*

We're of the friendly species 'octopus',
But of niceness we have not a jot,
Of ev'ry sea dweller we're jealous,
Particularly of Tumboo and Rot!

CHORUS: *Ohhh! They're jealous of Tumboo and Rot!*

Our hearts are like a sea lion's,
At least that's our heartfelt wish,
But if I didn't tell you I'd be lyin',
In our hearts we're just jellyfish!

CHORUS: *Ohhh! Jellyfish, they are jellyfish!*

Bullying sardines, for us, is a lark,
We'd gladly push around a shrimp,
But confront us with whale or shark,
And watch our tentacles go limp!

CHORUS: *Ohhh! Watch them go hopelessly limp!*

'Ha ha ha!' yelled Tumboo, her kilos quivering with helpless laughter.

Irrit, though, had a completely different opinion. He had already turned a delicate blue from lack of oxygen, but on hearing Po's vivid verse, he went bright purple! Fuming, he clapped three tentacles onto Po's beak, cutting off the stream of stanzas.

'That's q…quite enough, Po!'

'No, no,' Tumboo objected. This was the best laugh she'd had in days. 'Look! Even the shark's enjoying it!'

Which, strangely, seemed to be true. The fin was no longer slicing menacingly through the water. It was shaking and jerking all over the pool! This was a turn of events even Irrit couldn't ignore. Reluctantly, he unwound his tentacles from around Po's mouth. Instantly, the inspired poet took up from where he'd been cut off:

All we want is to be on the show,
Our names to see illuminated:
THE SHOWSTOPPERS—IRRIT AND PO!
But to work hard we're not 'inclinated'.

CHORUS: Ohhh! To be slackers they are 'inclinated'!

Not a talented bone in our body,
We're two useless, talentless drones,
But with an excuse we are ever ready:
'Octopuses, you know, have no bones!'

CHORUS: Ohhh! No talented bones, no bones!

Since we're untalented (and that's a fact),
We'll sabotage all other species,
Mess up everyone else's act,
And then gasp, pant, wheeze, wheeze…

'Wheeze, wheeze' wasn't a rhyme for *'species'*—Po had literally run out of breath! The deluge of doggerel sputtered and petered out. Po swayed and before Irrit could grab him, toppled right into the pool!

'H…help!' croaked Irrit. Breathless himself, he sagged to the ground, looking on in helpless horror as his buddy hit the water not five feet from the shark!

With the unconscious octopus at its mercy, the shark could have…

- raced in, carved Po up with razor-like teeth and swallowed him whole!

OR

~ grabbed Po and dragged him to the shark lair, to be shared among other hungry sharks!

Oddly, it did neither. The shark fin shivered and shuddered and suddenly burst out of the water. And below the fin there was NO SHARK! The fin was attached to a holder that was fastened to the halfway limb of an octopus who followed it out of the water, doubled over with laughter!

'Ha ha ha ha ha!' roared Rot. He hadn't been able to hold himself in anymore. 'Orca the whale-shark! That was terrific, Tumbs! Ha ha ha ha!'

'A nice touch, if I say so myself,' grinned Tumboo.

'A...and did you get those lyrics?' Rot hooted. '"*Octopuses, you know, have no bones!*" Sheer genius! That song's going to be the hit of the show!'

Tumboo guffawed and Irrit watched in disbelief as Rot let the air out of the inflatable fin.

'You...you...' Irrit gasped but, like Po, he had run out of the breath needed to express his feelings.

'Shove him into the water, Tumbs,' Rot said, still laughing. 'Let them get some oxygen into their gills.'

'Yeah!' grinned Tumboo. 'I want to know how that song ends.' She heaved Irrit into the pool and followed him in.

Cool, oxygen-rich water flowed through Irrit and Po's gills. Very quickly, Irrit was up and about, nasty as ever. Po, however, did not stir.

'He's dead!' barked Irrit, always ready to believe the worst. 'You've killed him!'

'No, we haven't,' Rot grinned. 'Tumbs, you're up!'

'What!' Tumboo exclaimed. 'You mean…?'

'Yep! The Kiss of Life!'

'But why must it always be me?'

'Go on, Tumbs,' Rot said, laughing at Tumboo's

disgusted expression. 'Who knows—this could be the start of a beautiful relationship!'

Looking as if she was about to bite into a particularly slimy sea slug, Tumboo placed her lips on Po's gills. In-and-out she blew water, in-and-out with all the force of her fifty kilos. In no time at all, Po's eyes fluttered open.

'Aaaahhh,' he sighed, 'that feels great!'

Instantly, Tumboo yanked her lips away.

'Blblblblblb,' she burbled, trying to get Po's taste off her lips.

'Ah, the kiss of true love!' said Rot, a wicked twinkle in his eye. 'Always works!'

'Blaahh!' Tumboo went, feeling like she didn't want anything to touch her lips for at least a week.

Of course, not a day elapsed before she changed her mind and happily tucked into her third breakfast. She *was* Tumboo, after all!

2

With just a week to go for the concert, Sea World was buzzing with excitement. Jai Kalia, chairman of the Octopus Group of Companies, was sponsoring the show and Zubair Midha, the famous music maestro, had agreed to be the Chief Guest. The pools were scrubbed down, the viewing areas were cleaned up, the waters sparkled (the defaced poster of the Oct-estra had been quickly replaced, the identity of the vandals remaining an unsolved mystery). Most importantly, the Oct-estra itself was smack in the middle of all this hectic activity—practising, practising, practising!

Throughout the day, melodious music wafted out from the Oct-estra chamber. The chamber itself was divided into two by a glass wall. On one side, the area was filled with water while the other side contained a platform for the Oct-estra conductor and a seating area for spectators. Delic8, Clarin8, Gyr8 and Pyr8 floated in the water-filled section, their specially designed underwater musical instruments poised, waiting for a signal from the conductor. On the dry side, standing on the conductor's platform, looking uncannily like a sparrow with her grey hair and brown cardigan, was a tiny, elderly human with glasses perched on her nose.

'Ready, dikra?' Ms Freni Birdy chirruped (Ms Birdy called everyone 'dikra', Gujarati for 'child').

She pointed her baton at the waterproof music sheets placed before the Oct-estra. The octopuses looked at the strange sheets covered with squiggles and wondered why the lady with the stick always pointed at them. The 'squiggles', of course, were music notations and these particular sheets contained directions for *Twinkle Twinkle Little Star*. The notations, however, were meaningless for the octopuses. They played entirely from memory, having picked up their melodies from the music they had heard in the lab of their favourite human: the vet, Dr Reena Renaldo. But the

octopuses liked Ms Birdy and always politely waited for her to wave her stick before they started playing. Ms Birdy gestured and the quartet launched into action.

Ms Birdy waved at Gyr8—and Clarin8 struck up his cello. Ms Birdy gestured at Delic8—and Pyr8 blew on his bassoon. Glorious music echoed in the chamber with a bewildered Ms Birdy desperately waving her baton, trying to keep up with the octopuses' playing. The moment the piece ended, the human listeners drawn into the chamber by the wonderful music broke into spontaneous applause.

'My favourite concerto!' Reena exclaimed. 'That was wonderful, Ms Birdy!'

'H'een-credi-bull!' cried Dr Zubbu Zwami. 'H'even better than yezterday'z Beethoven Zymphony!'

'Zubair Midha will be thrilled!' the Senior Supervisor gushed. 'How do you do it, Ms Birdy?'

Ms Birdy tittered nervously. 'I wonder what they played!' she thought to herself.

Behind her, the eight-limbed geniuses grinned.

'Let's play another piece!' said Pyr8. 'Something with snap!'

'Yeah!' Gyr8 echoed. 'The one with cannons!' she said, referring to the Tchaikovsky Overture.

'All right,' laughed their mother. 'But not too loud. The last time you fired the shot, the nice lady jumped right off her platform!'

Naturally, the show for Zubair Midha had generated huge interest and the media was clamouring for admission. But the chamber where the Oct-estra performed was too small for television cameras and crews—letting them in would mean crowding out Zubair Midha himself!

'If only we could get the cameras in,' sighed the Senior Supervisor. 'Just think of the publicity!'

'We could ftill do it, fir,' said the Junior Supervisor (who had a noticeable lisp). 'I have a folufion!'

'Folufion?' asked the Senior Super, confused.

'Fure, fir. Quite fimple, really! Eafy!'

'Eafy?'

'Feel!'

'Feel?'

The Junior Super looked pained. His boss obviously had not grasped his 'fimple folufion'. Eagerly, the Junior Super grabbed the Senior Super's arm.

'Feel!' he said, impatiently. 'Feel!'

The Senior Super looked nervously at his assistant. Was the man completely sane?

'Shoo!' he said, trying to wave away his grasping junior. 'Shoo!'

'Foo?'

'Shoo!'

Desperately, the Junior Super jabbed a finger in the direction of a platform bobbing in the middle of Sea World's vast Central Pool.

'There, fir!' he almost shouted. 'The floating ftage! Where the performing feel performf!'

'Performing...?' Light dawned on the Senior Super. 'Oh, *seal*! Performing seal!'

'That'f what I faid—feel!'

'What about it?' the Senior Super asked, soothingly.

'The floating ftage, fir,' the Junior Super said, enthusiastically. 'The octopufef could perform on it. There'f plenty of fpafe for the cameraf and ftuff here!' He pointed at the many-tiered spectators' galleries that surrounded the pool.

The Senior Super looked at the Junior Super.

'Now, why didn't I think of that?' said the Senior Super.

The Junior Super preened. His 'folufion' worked!

'Of course...' the Senior Super said.

'Of course'? Was there an 'of course'? thought the Junior Super, suddenly anxious.

'Of course, seals perform in the open air,' continued the Senior Super. 'Octopuses perform underwater.'

Underwater! The Junior Super could have kicked himself. He had forgotten that!

'Now all you have to do,' continued the Senior Super with a glint in his eye, 'is to train those octopuses to breathe air. You have seven days. Should be easy!'

Septopus

The Senior Super strode away leaving the Junior Super gaping after him in dismay. Seven days to train the octopuses to breathe air? It definitely was NOT 'eafy'!

What the Junior Super could not know, of course, was that Fate had something very interesting up its sleeve. Dr Reena Renaldo and Dr Zubbu Zwami had been conducting a series of experiments to determine smells that attracted water creatures. And since Rot was the most intelligent water creature they had ever seen, it was natural that Reena and Zubbu wanted Rot's opinion on the various smells they came up with. Different smells were added to food laid out before Rot and the octopus had the enviable task of choosing from a variety of delicious-smelling fare.

'But why not me?' complained Tumboo. 'No one knows more about food than me!'

'That's obvious!' Rot grinned.

'You tell the Lab Lady, Rot!' Tumboo urged. 'If she needs a food expert, I have the expertience…uh… expertession…er…I know it all!

'It's not about food, Tumbs,' explained Rot, patiently. 'It's about smells. I think they just want to know what smells good to us. And you know all food smells good to you!'

'Obviously! It's food! I'm going to protest! It's discrimitation…er…prejudation…uh…it's unfair!'

So the next time Rot went to Reena's lab, he took his protesting pal along. They went through the special pipe that connected the pool to the lab—the Hotline—and plopped into the lab's tank, but as neither Reena nor Zubbu was present, it clearly wasn't feed time. There did happen to be a human in the lab, however, a Sea World worker about whom there appeared to be nothing out of the ordinary except for the rather gaudy red-and-yellow sneakers he had on. The human was vacuuming the lab carefully, which was advisable considering the forest of delicate equipment around. His next actions, therefore, were quite unexpected. The human looked at the closed door, and then casually moved to a table, on top of which were four jars. These jars contained the food that the scientists had chemically treated so that each bit of food smelt different. And further, to ensure that the contents didn't get mixed up, the jars had differently coloured labels: red, blue, green and yellow. The worker, however, didn't differentiate. He deliberately toppled all four jars over, spilling their contents onto the tabletop.

'Oops!' said the human, a mocking smile playing on his thin lips.

Sweeping the spilt food into one pile, he carried the mixture to the tank and tossed it into the water.

'All yours, you stinkin' slugs!' he said rudely to Rot and Tumboo.

Then, whistling a carefree tune, he turned the jars upright and wheeled the vacuum cleaner out of the lab.

'Finally!' exclaimed Tumboo, hungrily eyeing the food that the worker had dropped into their tank. 'Let's dig in, Rot!'

'I'm not sure we should, Tumbs,' Rot said. 'The Lab Lady usually puts food in just one jar at a time.'

'She's not here, Rot! And the food *is*!' Tumboo put on a virtuous air. 'With so many fish going hungry, it's not right to waste food.'

Rot grinned. The four-food mixture smelt a little odd, but not unpleasant. Rot snapped a spoon onto his halfway limb and sampled the mixed-up food gingerly, noting the unusual smell and the interesting taste.

He nodded.

'You're right, Tumbs! Let's eat!'

Tumboo lost no time. Displaying astonishing vacuuming abilities herself, she swept over the food, inhaling everything edible. Shortly, all the food was relocated from the inside of the tank to the inside of Tumboo's stomach (apart from the few spoonfuls that Rot managed).

The tubby turtle settled back with a contented sigh. 'Now that's what I call breakfast!' she said.

Rot grinned. 'That was breakfast, lunch *and* dinner! We had all four jars, remember?'

'Well, I'm a healthy, growing turtle,' Tumboo remarked. 'My body needs the energy.'

In fact, Tumboo could feel the energy coursing through her ample body. Her skin tingled, her flippers prickled, her tail twitched. Strangely, Rot felt a similar sensation, too. From the top of his head to the tips of his tentacles he felt a stirring, as if he had touched a low-voltage electric eel. Suddenly, the tingling, the stirring, the prickling shot up to a new level. The friends gasped.

Their eyeballs spun, their limbs jerked wildly, they

were jolted all over the tank like hooked fish. Then they went completely rigid and…

CRASH!

'What was that?' Reena said, startled.

'Zomething in the lab!' said Zubbu.

They hurried down the corridor to the lab, threw open the door—and froze! The tank lay on the ground, overturned. Water streamed across the lab floor, dangerously soaking electrical points. But what caught the attention of the scientists was a turtle standing on the ground *on its hind feet*! It was their turtle, the one who stored the octopus' gadgets in her shell. Even as the scientists stood stunned for a moment, the turtle noticed them, started guiltily and spun around on her feet. Reena and Zubbu watched in disbelief as the turtle leapt towards the open window! And just as she became airborne, an octopus tentacle whipped forward. Not an ordinary tentacle, but a halfway limb with a clamp attached to it. The clamp hooked onto the turtle's shell and, as the turtle vaulted clean through the window, an octopus—their octopus—rode along, soaring out of the lab into the grounds outside!

3

'Do you know w-what you just d-did?' Rot asked Tumboo, as he was jarred and jounced around, hanging on to the fleeing turtle's back.

'Yeah!' Tumboo replied worriedly, her hind legs pumping as she sprinted through the grounds. 'I knocked over the tank!'

'Not th-that!' Rot said. 'You j-jumped out of the window and now you're r-running!'

'Well, I have to get away! I messed up!'

'But…' Rot began, then gave up. 'Where are you going?'

'Up that tree! I'm going to hide!'

'You're g-going to *climb a tree??*'

'Yeah!' replied Tumboo, still not catching on.

'They'll never think of looking for me up there!'

And before Rot could object, Tumboo grabbed hold of a coconut tree and shinned up like a turtle-shaped monkey!

'Phew,' sighed Tumboo, squatting on one of the palm tree's fronds high above the ground, catching her breath. 'Should be safe now.'

Rot detached his clamp and grabbed hold of the frond with his tentacles. He eyed his friend silently.

'What?' Tumboo asked, uncomfortable under the octopus' steady gaze.

'You really don't get it, do you?' Rot said.

'Of course I do,' Tumboo replied, looking superior. 'Well?'

'This has never happened before!' Tumboo said, excitedly.

'You said it!' Rot exclaimed. 'What are we going to do about it?'

'Easy! Just reach out and snap one off!'

'What?'

'The coconuts!' Tumboo said, pointing. 'We've never been so close to so many!' She reached forward and broke off a luscious-looking nut.

Rot slapped his head with a frustrated tentacle. 'Coconuts! Is that what you're thinking of?'

'Yeah, isn't it great?' grinned Tumboo, trying to crack open the tough nut. 'You think you can help with this?'

Shaking his head, Rot took the coconut, which was almost as big as he was. 'I'll need a knife,' he said.

Tumboo riffled through her shell. 'Knife...' she muttered. 'Let's see...K...K...K...'

'K?' Rot asked, pleasantly surprised that Tumboo had hit upon the correct first letter. 'Not "N" for "Nife"?'

'Of course not!' Tumboo said, disdainfully. 'It's a Kokonut knife, isn't it?' She pulled out a pouch and handed it over.

Grinning, Rot snapped on the pouch and whipped his halfway limb forward. It *was* a knife!

'One "Kokonut" coming up,' Rot said, cutting through the thick shell.

He passed the opened nut to Tumboo. The turtle took a bite, then another and...paused.

'Strange,' she muttered. She looked at the sweet, milky flesh of the coconut and her stomach turned over. She couldn't bear the thought of another bite! 'There's something weird going on, Rot!'

'Weird?' Rot said, arching a sarcastic eyebrow. 'Really?'

'Well, you know how observant I am,' Tumboo continued, failing to observe Rot's eyebrow. 'I feel too full to eat, can you believe it? I'm surprised you don't find that odd, Rot!'

Rot grinned at her. Of course it was odd, strange, weird! And what was even more peculiar was the fact that he, Rot, was also a part of this. He knew that octopuses could survive only a few minutes out of water, and yet here he was, breathing normally, perched calmly atop a tree with Tumboo!

'How do you feel right now, Tumbs?'

'Full,' Tumboo replied. 'Full of air like a balloon! You may not have noticed, Rot, but I'm sometimes considered heavy (Rot suppressed a grin). But right now I feel light, as if I have no weight at all. I feel like I could run or jump or just float away!'

Full of air! That was exactly what Rot felt, too. The strange four-food mixture that Tumboo and he had eaten in the lab—it had triggered this extraordinary reaction. He understood now. Despite being a water-breather, Rot had suddenly developed the ability to breathe oxygen from the air. And Tumboo, who was already an air-breather, had so much air in her body now that she felt as light as a bubble!

'You're right, Tumbs,' Rot said. 'It *is* weird! I wonder what the Lab Lady and her friend would have to say about all this.'

∽

'H'een-credi-bull!' exclaimed Zubbu, looking up from his microscope. 'The h'octopuz' zkin haz developed porez! He can breathe h'oxygen from the h'air through hiz zkin!'

'And the turtle has so many pores now that the air entering her body has quadrupled!' Reena said, gazing into her microscope.

An hour ago, the scientists had been astounded to find Rot and Tumboo up a tree. The water creatures had been coaxed down and despite Reena and Zubbu's concerns about Rot, the octopus and turtle had scuttled along in the open air across the grounds to the lab. Through a series of gestures and a lot of

Septopus

pointing at the toppled jars, Rot had explained what had happened to the amazed scientists. And now, after having examined the water creatures, Zubbu made a beeline for the food, hoping to reproduce the four-food mixture.

'We have to find the egzact quantitiez!' he said, excitedly. 'H'imagine what h'it would mean h'if we could make h'all water creaturez breathe h'air!'

'Wait, Zubbu!' Reena said firmly. She looked worriedly at Rot and Tumboo. 'I want to check something first.'

Gently, she lifted the water creatures (surprisingly, lifting Tumboo wasn't difficult at all) and placed them on the ramp leading into the restored water tank. Happily, Rot and Tumboo scurried into the water. Rot eagerly sank below the water surface, letting the cool water stream through his gills. But his gills were not the only place into which the water flowed—his newly porous skin allowed water in everywhere! Rot felt his body bloating, bursting with water! And Tumboo was experiencing exactly the same horrible feeling. Though the turtle didn't breathe through gills, the water gushed through her porous skin, too. Rot and

Tumboo floundered, thrashed about, felt they were drowning! Reena and Zubbu watched, horrified, and rushed forward to help. But before they could reach the tank, Rot and Tumboo, gasping and straining, managed to drag themselves out of the water and onto the ramp.

'They can't breathe in the water!' cried Reena, looking at the panting water creatures, appalled. 'This is awful, Zubbu! We have to find a way to reverse what's happened to them!'

Of course, what Rot and Tumboo heard was: '… reovoersoo whiaatsee haoppoenieedo oto athoemoo!'

But despite the gibberish, the water creatures understood exactly what the humans were saying. Rot and Tumboo looked at each other, dismayed. They were marooned out of the water! Tumboo, perhaps, could still meet her parents out of the pools, but what about Rot? Had he lost his family, his home, forever?

༄

Two kilometres up the coast from Goa Sea World was another home—if indeed a palace could be called a home. With its private beach, manicured lawns and

Septopus

one hundred and six opulent rooms, Casa Octopusa was the most luxurious mansion in Goa. And in one of those one hundred and six rooms, seated on the edge of an expensive antique chair was a man wearing red-and-yellow sneakers. The door opened and the man sprang to his feet. The polished wooden floor creaked with the effort of supporting the weight of the man who entered. The newcomer strongly resembled a school bus, his enormously fat frame encased in a

bright yellow, octopus-print shirt. His salt-and-pepper hair and moustache set off a florid complexion and diamonds flashed on his podgy fingers and earlobes. One earring, though, was momentarily hidden by the cell phone he held against his ear.

'Sea World will be out of business in a month,' he said into the phone in a deep baritone. 'Then we'll take it over and tear it down. It's the perfect site for our new hotel.' He listened for a moment and grimaced. 'Yes, yes, don't worry. Your money's safe with me!' Disconnecting, he looked at the man standing before him. 'I hope you have good news,' he growled.

'Yes, sir,' said the man in red-and-yellow sneakers, clearing his throat nervously. 'I've started mixin' up de water creatures' food. Dey'll get sick for sure! Started with de octopus food first, like you wanted, Mr Kalia.'

Jai Kalia laughed. In business circles, Jai Kalia was known as 'The Octopus' since his empire's tentacles spread everywhere, grasping at any opportunity to make ill-gotten money. Kalia didn't find the label insulting at all. In fact, he had changed his company's name to 'The Octopus Group' and splashed its octopus symbol all over. Which was why Kalia laughed. It was amusing that his plan to destroy Sea World began with an attack on the octopuses. Kalia knew that the octopuses, and the Oct-estra in particular, were Goa Sea World's most popular attractions. He had sponsored the upcoming concert and persuaded Zubair Midha to attend it to ensure the presence of the media. Now all he had to do was to sabotage the show: the resulting fiasco would cause Sea World to collapse like a house of cards! No one would suspect that he, the sponsor, had anything to do with it. It was the perfect plan! 'The Octopus' laughed long and hard.

4

Irrit was worried about Po. Ever since the incident with Rot's inflatable shark fin, Po wasn't the nasty little octopus he used to be. Whenever Irrit tried to get his poetic pal interested in one of his slimy schemes, Po showed a disturbing lack of enthusiasm. Just the other day, Irrit had wanted to glue together their teacher Ms Noriko's lobster claws. But when he had mentioned the plan to Po, the latter had just sighed and looked away. What was wrong with him? Irrit decided he had to do something to snap his moping buddy out of his stupor. Irrit swam to the reef where Po and he usually hung out and as he neared it, he heard a deep sigh. Irrit stopped. That sounded like Po, a very gloomy Po. Irrit edged forward, peered around an outcrop and saw...Po sitting on a ledge, dejected, a soggy water lily in his tentacle.

'She loves me,' sighed Po, plucking a petal from the flower. 'She loves me not!' groaned the wretched rhymester, yanking off the last petal.

Irrit reeled. Po was in love! But who was the female octopus who had stolen his buddy's three hearts? Kissmek8? Firstd8? Hotpl8?

Po sniffed the petal-less flower's stem and suddenly, in a broken voice, droned:

Jyotin Goel

When she calls me 'Rogue' and 'Rotter',
My three hearts just leap and run,
When she displaces all that water,
I just know that she's the one!

Yes, she's the one for me!

My suckers did lose their suction,
When she called me 'jug of jelly',
I shivered from crown to cross-section,
When she jiggled that bountiful belly!

Yes, she's the one for me!

Holding me, on my gills she did kiss me,
Like being enfolded in a large, green tent,
My ink-gland took off like a frisbee
And I don't know where my funnel went!

Oh, she's the one for me!

All I want is to touch and tickle
Every one of her hundred-plus pounds,
Wrap her with my eight tentacles,
Though I'm not sure that they'll go around.

But she's the one for me!

Irrit was shocked, stunned, dumbfounded! He knew the object of Po's soppy sonnet—that 'large, green tent'.

'Tumboo!' he exclaimed.

Po started and turned. Irrit shot forward to confront the lovesick loser.

'Tumboo?' he barked at Po. 'You're in love with that two-ton turtle??'

Po sighed deeply and nodded, sniffing his drooping flower stem.

'Are you nuts, Po?' shouted Irrit. 'You're an octopus! Tumboo's a turtle!'

'But what a turtle!' Po said, adoringly.

'You can't fall for her just because she blew into your gills!'

'But what a kisser!'

'You've got water on the brain! Germs in your gelatin! Sand in your...'

Irrit stopped. He looked at his friend closely. Po had a faraway look in his eyes. Irrit's reproaches had washed over him with no effect at all. This was bad! Po was in danger of crossing over to the enemy—to Tumboo, and through her to Rot! Irrit had to prevent that. But what could he do? Suddenly, Irrit went still. A brilliantly evil idea surged into his mind. He could use Po, take advantage of his besotted buddy to wreck the Oct-estra, something he'd wanted to do for a long, long time!

'On second thought, Po,' Irrit said reasonably, 'maybe I'm wrong. Maybe a turtle *could* fall for an octopus…'

Po's faraway look vanished and he turned eagerly towards his crafty friend. 'You think so, Irrit?' he asked hopefully. 'You really think so?'

'Yeah,' Irrit replied. 'Look at Tumboo and Rot. Everyone thinks they're just friends, but I think there's more to it!'

'Tumboo and *Rot?*' repeated Po, shocked.

'Don't you see how they look at each other, how they're always together?' continued Irrit, cunningly. 'I wouldn't call that friendship, would you?'

'No…' breathed Po. 'No, I wouldn't…'

Octopuses can change colour and, as jealousy shot through Po, he turned as green as the flower stem he held. His tentacle whipped out angrily, sending the stem spinning through the water.

'It's always Rot!' he hissed. 'It's because of him she doesn't know I'm alive!'

'That's easily put right,' Irrit said, soothingly. 'All we have to do is sabotage the Oct-estra before the show for Zubair Midha.'

'And how would that help?' Po snapped.

'It's obvious! If the Oct-estra can't play, someone else would have to go onstage.'

'Someone...else?'

'As Tumboo herself put it,' Irrit said slyly, '"Po, you have a way with words!" You're the school poet. Who else could go on but you?'

Po's face lit up. 'And then she'd notice me!'

'Exactly!'

Irrit wasn't an octopus who let seaweed grow under his feet. Now that he had tricked Po into getting on board, he put his plan into operation immediately. Po, of course, was vital, but Irrit needed a few extra hands (or tentacles) to make his evil scheme work. It didn't take much persuasion to recruit Imit8 and Emul8 (two of Irrit's many cousins) since Imit8 wanted to be just like Irrit and Emul8 wanted to be just like Imit. Three sniggering octopuses (and one seething poet) stole through the dark water of the Oct-estra chamber. Music practice was over for the evening and Irrit knew there would be no one around to foil his nefarious designs. Quickly, the gang went to work, snapping open cases and extracting the specially designed underwater musical instruments.

'Hee hee,' sniggered Irrit.

'Hee hee,' sniggered Imit8, imitating Irrit.

'Hee hee,' sniggered Emul8, emulating Imit.

Po just glowered, not saying a word (which was quite a change)!

Gathering up the instruments, the gang bore them away out of the Oct-estra chamber into the pools beyond. Shortly, they reached Clam Cove. And this is where Po came into play—for he had a fan in this mob of molluscs: a giant clam called Sesame.

The massive shellfish had a dark corner of the lair all to himself. He was truly huge, five feet across, more than two hundred kilos of hard bulk. Like all clams, Sesame was close-mouthed, very, very frugal with words. It was impossible to prise open his enormous shells when he clamped them shut. No one could get a word out of the silent shellfish—except Po. The

poet was everything the clammed-up clam wanted to be: talkative, witty, fun! In fact, one could even hear Sesame rumble when Po was around, the closest he came to laughter. Po was the only one who could get Sesame to open up, to loosen his tightly clenched jaws.

And this was exactly what Irrit was counting on. Weighed down by their purloined instruments, the gang struggled up to the clam.

'Open, Sesame,' said Po.

The clam's huge shell rumbled open in a gargantuan 'Ah'. Irrit signalled and the gang loaded the instruments into the vast clam mouth.

'Zip the lip, Sesame,' said Po.

The octopuses backed away in a hurry, just in time to avoid the gigantic jaws as they crashed shut. The musical instruments vanished from sight as if they had never existed.

'Hee hee hee,' sniggered Irrit.
'Hee hee hee,' sniggered Imit.
'Hee hee hee,' sniggered Emul.
And even Po smiled!

5

'Mrs Turn Turtle,' said Delic8 in fractured Fishy (hardly anyone spoke it well), 'have seen Tumboo and Rot around?'

Rot's mom hadn't seen Rot for some time now, and was getting worried. Since Rot and Tumboo were practically inseparable, Delic8 had decided to approach Tumboo's mom about her concerns.

'No, but not worry,' Mrs Turn Turtle replied. 'You know how they went out of Sea World to other park last time!' she laughed. 'They show up soon, I sure!'

But Delic8 wasn't so sure. After Rot's last absence, he had made it a point to tell his mother if he and Tumboo were going to be busy with something. And this time he hadn't said a thing to her. So it was an uneasy Delic8 who accompanied her family to the

Oct-estra chamber for the day's practice session.

Rot was sure his mother was worried. He had been stuck out of the water for a night and a morning now and hadn't been able to tell his family what had occurred. Of course, other turtles would eventually emerge from the water and get the news from Tumboo, but Rot had no idea when that would happen. He *had* to meet his family right away and Rot knew just where: the Oct-estra chamber, the one place his family was sure to be since it practised there every day. There was a problem, however—his parents and siblings would be in the water-filled side of the chamber and Rot would be all alone on the dry side, a sturdy glass wall separating him from his family. At the thought, a lump formed in his throat and he felt a hot stinging in his eyes. But Rot was made of tough stuff. Until the Lab Lady and her friend came up with something that would enable him to breathe underwater again, he would just have to get used to being homeless. He swallowed hard, raised his head, and scuttled into Sea World's grounds, heading for the Oct-estra chamber.

Normally, Rot would have glided smoothly through

the water down a series of pipes and popped up next to his family behind the glass wall of the Oct-estra chamber. But things had changed. He was an air-breather now and a five-minute walk in the open air for an octopus (even an air-breathing one) was no stroll in the park. Rot knew how delicious he looked to birds—a moving bowl of mouth-watering jelly with seven (and-a-half) thick, juicy worms attached! If he was going to walk around in the open, Rot was going to have to protect himself from overhead attacks.

BRR-APP!!

Rot whipped his halfway limb forward and snapped open an umbrella! He grinned; it was a simple solution for his problem. Getting the umbrella, though, had not been all that simple. The attachments for his halfway limb were in Tumboo's shell, but finding her was no easy matter. Ever since she had eaten that strange food mixture in the lab, the turtle had lost her appetite, downing just one breakfast instead of the four she did earlier. So upset was she with this state of affairs that she had taken to disappearing between mealtimes. Rot had managed to track her down, stumbling across the turtle frowsting glumly under a bush. Rot mentioned the umbrella and Tumboo reached listlessly into her shell, pulling out the first pouch she touched. Rot raised a sceptical eyebrow. Tumboo rarely picked the correct pouch even when searching carefully—with his friend in this mood they'd probably find the umbrella just in time for the monsoons! Dubiously, Rot attached it to his tentacle, snapped it forward and out sprang: an umbrella!

'I don't believe it!' Rot exclaimed, astonished.

'Sorry,' Tumboo said, not even looking. 'Ever since I lost my appetite, nothing's going right.'

'But it *is* right! You got it, first go!'

'Did I? Lucky me,' Tumboo sighed wistfully.

Rot grinned. Tumboo would definitely disagree, but the mixed-up food had some benefits, after all!

And so here was Rot, protected from above, scurrying along under his parasol like a miniature Mary Poppins. The thing about being an octopus is that one is only a foot tall. Therefore, the umbrella that Rot carried was travelling along just over a foot above the ground. Its edges curved downward (the way umbrella edges do) so that Rot's view was restricted to whatever was visible up to a height of nine inches. Of course, there are hundreds of things to be seen even within this limited view and the first thing Rot became aware of was the number of creepy-crawlies that populated Sea World's lawns and pathways. Neatly, Rot sidestepped a slow-moving slug and vaulted over a line of quick-marching ants. There were a fair number of humans too, though all Rot could see of them were the hems of saris or the legs of trousers. The owners of the saris and trousers seemed astonished at the sight of an umbrella apparently moving along all by itself. Repeatedly, human faces dipped into Rot's nine-inches-above-the-ground view, looking shocked or amused at coming face-to-face with an air-breathing, umbrella-toting octopus!

Refusing to be distracted, Rot soldiered on, hurrying to meet his family. Suddenly, a pair of human feet swept past. Rot stopped, startled. His eyes narrowed, as the feet shod in red-and-yellow sneakers drew rapidly away. He had seen those gaudy shoes earlier and he knew exactly where: in the Creature Lab on the feet of the man who had mixed up their food! Rot's eyes locked on to a green food pail that jolted along next to the man's feet. There

was nothing unusual about the pail itself—similar pails were carried by keepers all over Sea World, containing food for the water creatures. But there was something here that Rot instinctively disliked, though he couldn't put a tentacle on it. The man was moving fast and quickly disappeared around a corner. A sliver of food, though, had slopped out of the pail and lay on the grass a few metres ahead. A seagull looked at it curiously and hopped closer. Rot hustled forward, his umbrella spooking the bird, who squawked and flew off. Rot looked at the finger-length of food. It looked completely normal (quite delicious, in fact), but Rot wasn't satisfied. He had very sensitive smell receptors in all his tentacles, almost as if he had seven-and-a-half noses. And those 'noses' were twitching, picking up a very faint odour almost hidden by the scent of the food. Gingerly, Rot dipped a tentacle into the slop and raised it to his beak. He rolled the speck of food around in his mouth. No…he couldn't taste anything unusual. But he trusted his sense of smell—even the Lab Lady had done so. Decisively, Rot spat out the morsel and scrambled towards the Oct-estra chamber.

Meanwhile, the chamber itself was a scene of utter confusion.

'But who could have done this?' demanded Delic8, staring at the empty cello and trumpet cases.

'And why would anyone take our instruments?!' Clarin8 exclaimed, snapping open a viola case and finding it empty, too.

Gyr8 and Pyr8 flitted furiously from case to looted case.

'It's got to be Irrit!' Gyr8 seethed.

'And Po!' added Pyr8, outraged.

Ms Birdy hopped from one foot to the other on the conductor's dais, looking through the glass wall at the flustered octopuses. All at once, she understood what was bothering the quartet—the musical instruments were missing!

The outer door banged open and a surly-looking keeper barged in (wearing red-and-yellow sneakers).

'Sorry, dikra,' Ms Birdy called out. 'Practice time. You can't come in now and do ting-ting in the middle!'

'Lunch!' announced the newcomer, raising a food pail.

'Oh!' Ms Birdy reacted. Was it already time for a break? 'Er…could you help us, dikra?' she asked the keeper timidly. 'Our instruments seem to have been misplaced.'

'Don't know nutting 'bout dat!' the keeper replied unhelpfully.

Yanking open the lid to the feeding chute, he poured in the contents of the pail, the food sliding into the water-filled side of the Oct-estra chamber, just a few feet from the agitated octopuses…

6

Rot had just reached the Oct-estra chamber's door when it swung outward. It slammed into his umbrella and knocked him off his feet, sending him tumbling onto the path outside. Sprawled on the gravel, Rot caught a fleeting glimpse of red-and-yellow sneakers as they flashed past. There was no apology from the owner of those shoes, no outstretched hand to help the flattened octopus to his feet.

'Not a very nice human,' Rot thought, as he watched the man stride away.

But he didn't waste time grumbling about human lack of manners. Rot was anxious to be with his family and he hurriedly struggled upright and stepped into the Oct-estra chamber.

'Mom!'

Delic8 stopped. She had been reaching for the food lying below the feeding chute when she heard her son's voice. She spun around and there he was: her missing son, smiling at her from under an umbrella, impossibly standing in the open-air section of the Oct-estra chamber!

'Rot!' breathed Delic8. 'Son!'

The unexpected arrival of food a few minutes ago had distracted the quartet from its frantic search of the empty instrument cases. And they had just been about to eat when they heard Rot's voice.

'Dad! Guys!' shouted Rot, grinning madly, scurrying towards the glass wall.

'Oh!' twittered Ms Birdy, thoroughly confused.

From atop her conductor's platform, all she could see was an umbrella moving along on its own.

'Um…er…' stuttered Ms Birdy, wondering how to address an umbrella. Should she call out 'Umbrella'? But that was bad manners. After all, calling out 'Man' to a man or 'Woman' to a woman was not the done thing! She chose the only way out. 'Dikra,' she said politely to the umbrella. 'Practice time. You can't come in now and do ting-ting in the middle!'

Septopus

But the umbrella seemed to have a mind of its own, ignoring Ms Birdy and rolling on towards the glass partition. And the octopuses on the other side rushed to meet the disobedient umbrella!

'Rot!'

'Son!'

'Hey, bro!'

'Dude, where've you been?'

WHR-CHK!

Rot folded his umbrella down and Ms Birdy suddenly understood. So that's what it was, she thought. Just an octopus carrying an umbrella. How foolish of her to think that there was something unusual happening!

The octopuses crowded together on the opposite sides of the glass wall.

'Why are you on that side, son?' asked Clarin8.

'How can you breathe?' Delic8 asked, really worried for her son. 'Are you all right?'

Rot pressed against the glass. He felt terrible that he couldn't reach out and touch his family, but he put on a brave face. 'Don't worry about me, Mom, Dad, guys,' he said. 'I can breathe just fine!'

'But how?' asked Gyr8 and Pyr8 together.

'Weird story,' replied Rot. 'Tumboo and I were in the lab and the food…'

Rot stopped. He had just noticed the food lying on the floor below the feeding chute. His eyes widened, his octopus alarm jangled! The food, its texture, its colour; it looked very similar to the morsel of food that had fallen out of the food pail that man had been carrying, that mouthful that had made him so suspicious!

'But Rot,' Clarin8 went on, 'are you sure…'

'Dad! Mom!' Rot interrupted. 'That food! Have any of you guys eaten it?'

'What…?'

'The food on the floor! I hope you haven't…'

'No…' Delic8 said, uncertainly. 'We were just about to start when you came in…'

'Yeah!' Gyr8 said. 'I just had a nibble…'

'Or two…' added Pyr8.

'Don't eat any more!' Rot cut in. 'There could be something wrong with it. And Mom, Dad, save some of it before the keepers clean it out. If it's actually bad, the Lab Lady will want to take a look!'

'But where are you going?'

'The man who brought it,' Rot replied. 'He needs to answer a few questions!'

He scurried to the door, snapped open his umbrella and rushed out.

Following Rot's instructions, the four octopuses scooped up some of the suspect food and poured it into the empty music cases. Ms Birdy watched in astonishment.

'You know, that's very clever,' she tittered. 'I must remember to carry a bigger handbag the next time I'm invited to a Navjot dinner!'

Rot looked around. There were hundreds of humans all over Sea World. Where was the man who had brought the food? Rot scuttled forward. Being a highly intelligent octopus, he had noticed that humans stuck to marked pathways, avoiding lawns. Why they did so baffled Rot. Why on earth would humans avoid grass (which was so much softer on one's tentacles) and choose to walk on hard tar or gravel instead? Humans were strange, indeed. Their odd behaviour, though, was lucky for Rot. By choosing to walk on hard surfaces, humans were forced to wear shoes. And

Septopus

that's what Rot was tracking. The limited view he had from under the umbrella didn't bother him. He didn't have to look at the faces of the hundreds of humans around. All he had to do was find a pair of feet shod in red-and-yellow sneakers. Rot darted over the grass, staring at the adjacent paths, checking out hundreds of feet tramping on tar, gravel and flagstone.

Exactly one hundred and four metres ahead of Rot, moving briskly down a winding path, were the very shoes that Rot was tracking. The path beyond had just been surfaced and the tar had yet to dry. A worker was placing a prominent sign warning visitors to 'KEEP OFF THE PATH'. Unfortunately, the worker was Claude Custado, the clumsiest attendant in Sea World. He stepped back to admire his handiwork and his eye fell on another sign that stood on the lawn next to the path: it said 'KEEP OFF THE GRASS'. Clumsy Claude was stumped. How could anyone keep off the path and the grass at the same time? It wasn't possible. But then Claude noticed something: a narrow flowerbed filled with brightly coloured flowers running between the path and the lawn. To Claude's wondrous brain, it was the perfect solution! Quickly, he picked up the 'KEEP OFF THE PATH' sign, laid it flat on the edge of the flowerbed and started squeezing an additional message on to the sign.

Claude had just finished his task when he heard a grunt of annoyance. He looked around and saw that an unbelievably clumsy person, another Sea World attendant, had blundered onto the path. The man had tracked footprints onto the freshly laid tar, ruining it, and was actually glaring at Claude as if it were *his* fault! Self-righteously, Claude held up his newly altered sign:

> KEEP OFF THE PATH
> *and Graas, and Waulk*
> *on the Flourbed Insted*

Angrily, the man looked at his shoes. The red-and-yellow sneakers had tar all over their soles. If he walked any further in them, they would be completely ruined. Gingerly, the man hopped into the flowerbed, took off his shoes, popped them into the empty food pail he carried, scowled angrily at Claude and, in his socks, stomped off over the lawn, completely ignoring the very clear instructions on Claude's sign!

Septopus

Rot was frustrated. He had searched all over Sea World, but nowhere had he come across any human wearing red-and-yellow sneakers. Rot wasn't prepared to give up, though.

'I need a wider view,' he thought.

⁓

'Coconut tree?' Tumboo was indignant. 'Don't talk to me about coconut trees! If I never see another coconut in my life, it'll be too soon!' She shut her eyes firmly, pretending to sleep.

Despite himself, Rot grinned. For Tumboo, her loss of appetite was tragic, but Rot found it hilarious! However, this was no time for hilarity. The man with red-and-yellow sneakers had to be tracked down and for that they needed to look far and wide from atop a coconut tree.

'Listen, Tumbs,' Rot said, 'the attendant who mixed up our food in the lab… I'm sure this is the same man. I think someone's trying to mess up Sea World. We have to stop them!'

Tumboo yawned.

Rot looked at her and continued, 'Anyway, it's the only chance of getting your appetite back.'

Tumboo's eyes snapped open. 'Why are we wasting time?' she exclaimed. 'You may not realize this, Rot, but it's our duty to save Sea World!'

Barely hiding a grin, Rot hooked his umbrella onto Tumboo's shell as the suddenly energized turtle raced to a tall coconut tree and streaked up its trunk like a fat lizard. Reaching the top, Tumboo's eyes alighted upon all the sweet, succulent nuts surrounding her. Her new-found enthusiasm leaked out like air from an overfilled balloon.

'Coconuts, coconuts everywhere with all their milky meat! Coconuts, coconuts everywhere and not a bite to eat!' she thought, lamenting like an old sailor starving on a deserted island.

'Binoculars, Tumbs,' said Rot.

Tumboo handed over the correct pouch.

'What?' Rot remarked, grinning. 'No "Ball", "Brick" or "Burger"?'

Tumboo just sighed deeply.

Rot snapped the field glasses onto his halfway tentacle and raised them to his eyes. From the top of the tree, Rot had a bird's-eye view of Sea World's grounds.

But despite his sharp octopus vision, enhanced by powerful binocular lenses, Rot was unable to zero in on the missing red-and-yellow shoes. He swivelled the binoculars, focusing and refocusing and…stopped. What had he just seen? He swung the glasses around and zoomed in on a path. There was no mistake. Right in the middle of the tarred surface were prints made by sneaker soles. The prints headed off the path into a flowerbed. There were traces of tar on the crushed flowers. But there were no prints heading back onto the path and *no traces of tar on the grass* of the lawn on the other side of the flowerbed! Instantly, Rot understood. The man had removed his shoes and walked away over the grass. An image sprang into Rot's mind: a pair of feet clad only in socks that had passed him barely fifteen minutes ago. Rot's smell receptors twitched at the memory. Those socks were the smelliest human-wear he had ever smelt! And if the man in the smelly socks was the same man who had taken off his tarred sneakers, then it was very possible that those sneakers were...

'C'mon, Tumbs! Let's go!'

But Tumboo was busy winding palm fronds around a bunch of coconuts.

Rot was baffled. 'What are you doing, Tumbs?'

'Tying them to the tree,' replied Tumboo. 'Falling coconuts are dangerous!'

'Ah!' Rot said, a twinkle in his eye. 'Nothing to do with keeping them up here until you get your appetite back?'

'That's rude!' Tumboo reacted, trying to look hurt. 'It's our duty to protect everyone from falling coconuts!'

Septopus

'All right.' Rot settled down. 'Let me know when you're done. I think I've got a lead on the man who's going to help you get your appetite back.'

'Well, why didn't you say so?' Tumboo leapt up. 'It's our duty to get this man to my appetite…uh…to back my man's appetite…I mean…to get this man's appetite back!'

7

Rot peered through the magnifying glass he had fastened to his halfway limb. The shoe prints on the path were very clear and so were the streaks of tar in the flowerbed. But what was even more distinct was the smell that the man's socks had trailed in the grass. To the super-sensitive smell receptors in Rot's tentacles (his seven-and-a-half noses), it was almost as if someone had painted arrows on the ground, marking the route the man had taken. Rot didn't need a magnifying glass to shadow his quarry. Instead, hooking his halfway limb onto Tumboo's shell with a clamp, he hitched a ride and trailed his tentacles on the ground, sniffing out the odour, tracking the man's footsteps over the lawn.

'Even I can smell that!' Tumboo asserted. 'I'm sure

I could do the job for the Lab Lady, smelling the food!'

'Yeah, but what good is food to you now?'

Tumboo said nothing, just sighed gloomily.

Shortly, they found themselves at the border of the lawn where it opened out into a wide, hard-surfaced area. This was where humans kept all those machines in which they travelled from place to place. Tracking the smell, Rot and Tumboo moved quickly and then… there they were, the smelly socks, on feet that were climbing into the front cabin of one of those travelling machines! They couldn't clearly see the man who belonged to the feet as his upper body was already in the cabin. Even as they watched, the man emptied the red-and-yellow sneakers from a food pail through the rear window of the cabin into the open back of the machine. Then he started the engine.

'He's triggered the machine!' Rot knew what followed when humans did that. 'He's going to get away!'

'But then…what about my appetite?' demanded Tumboo. 'I'll stop him!'

And before Rot could get a word in, she ran forward right into the path of the moving van!

Septopus

Standing upright, Tumboo raised a stern flipper at the oncoming vehicle.

'Estoppo!' she shouted, remembering a line from a cartoon movie that had a similar situation. 'Yooeaarie oounderaa restoo!'

Actually, the movie line was, 'Stop! You're under arrest!' but Tumboo was close enough. Unfortunately for the turtle, her dramatic line had no effect at all. The van picked up speed and hurtled right at her. And clamped onto Tumboo's shell was Rot, a completely unwilling accomplice in her heroics! In a flash, Rot

unhitched himself from the clamp and swung around to face his fat, foolhardy friend.

'Move, Tumbs!' he shouted.

Too late. The front grill of the van struck Rot smack in the middle of his back, driving him into Tumboo. The turtle was knocked down but instinctively rolled over and yanked her limbs into her shell. The wheel of the charging van struck Tumboo's hard carapace and bounced straight up. For a moment, the van teetered, then the wheel hit the ground again and the vehicle squealed away through the car park gate. Tumboo's head popped out of her shell.

'Phew, that was close!' she panted, watching the van race away. 'He's gone. What do we do now, Rot?' There was no reply. 'Rot? Rot?'

'Zx...vbny...sdfug...klo...qiw...' A feeble sound struggled up.

'Rot?' Tumboo looked around. 'Is that you? Where...?'

'Wiq...olk...gufds...ynbv...xz...'

Suddenly, Tumboo realized where the sound was coming from. She jerked upright, onto her hind feet. Spread flat on the hard tarmac where Tumboo lay a moment ago was an octopus-shaped inkblot. Could that splatter be Rot? It must be, since the strange sounds appeared to be emerging from it. Tumboo remembered that octopuses have this wonderful ability to copy any surface with which they come in contact. So that's what Rot was doing! He was mimicking the road!

'That's terrific, Rot!' said Tumboo, all admiration. 'How do you do it?'

How did he do it? Simple! Lie flat on a concrete road with a rock-hard turtle shell on top and get a two-ton van to run over the turtle! Rot's feelings were too deep for words. Painfully, he detached himself from the road surface and stood up, trying to stretch himself, looking very peculiar. His jelly-like

body was stamped with impressions of the surfaces against which he had been squished. His front was the spitting image of the ridges and curves of Tumboo's shell. But it was his back that was decidedly odd. Right in the middle, where the grill of the van had struck Rot, was a deep mark that looked like an octopus!

It was embarrassing, of course, for Rot to scuttle about with a turtle tattooed all over his front. But it was even more awkward for an octopus to have an octopus engraved on his back! Fortunately, the marks and indentations didn't last very long on Rot's body. He had no bones to break and his elastic skin just snapped back to normal.

But even though the marks disappeared, Rot's worries didn't. His misgivings were confirmed: Gyr8 and Pyr8, who had nibbled at the suspicious food, had been laid up with upset stomachs. Reena had analysed the food that the octopuses had saved and was horrified to find it contaminated—if the octopuses had eaten more, they would have been seriously ill!

'There's no way they would have been able to play in the concert,' Reena informed the Senior Supervisor the next day.

The Senior Super laughed—a hollow, doleful sound. 'Concert?' he moaned. 'What concert? The Oct-estra's specially designed underwater instruments have disappeared! Why does everything happen to me?'

Everything indeed did seem to be conspiring against him. Even in his own office he had no peace. A vacuum cleaner was buzzing insistently in the corner, its sound pounding on the Senior Super's temples. Exasperated, he waved at the worker who was trundling the machine around. The man nodded, switched off the maddening contraption and wheeled it out. But the sudden silence didn't improve the Senior Super's mood.

'Definitely not my day!' he groaned as he noticed the traces of tar left on his new carpet by the worker's ugly red-and-yellow sneakers.

On the other hand, Gyr8 and Pyr8 were feeling much better.

'There you go,' Dr Reena Renaldo cooed, slipping the two young octopuses into the tank where Delic8 and Clarin8 anxiously waited. In a moment, the youngsters were wrapped in loving parental tentacles.

'Aw, Mom,' Pyr8 protested. 'Enough, already! I'm fine!'

It was lucky they were underwater and Delic8's happy tears were not visible or Pyr8 would have been even more embarrassed!

Rot stood on a table next to Reena, happily watching his reunited family.

'They've completely recovered,' Reena said to Rot and pointed to a vial on the table. 'It's this amazing new medicine. It works wonders on octopuses!'

Then she laughed at herself. Rot was so intelligent she often talked to him, forgetting he couldn't understand her. Smiling, she patted Rot and left the room. Reena was mistaken, though. Rot may not have followed her words but he had clearly understood their meaning. Rot, however, wasn't thinking about the amazing octopus medicine. He was still stranded in the open air, forced apart from his parents and siblings. Watching his happy family, his eyes grew moist and he roughly brushed away the tear that formed. Delic8 had noticed, however, and she floated forward, her worried gaze on her son, stuck indefinitely out of the water.

Septopus

'Are you all right, son?' she asked through the acrylic wall of the tank.

'I'm good, Mom!' Rot forced a smile. 'Great to see the Oct-estra together again!'

'Yeah,' Pyr8 agreed, gliding up, 'but what's the use of an Oct-estra without instruments?'

'It's got to be that Irrit who's taken them!' Gyr8 looked seriously annoyed.

'And Po!' Pyr8 added.

'They just make me so mad!' Gyr8 fumed.

'Shush, child,' Clarin8 said. 'I'm sure those instruments will turn up. We're just happy you're well again.'

'But they're not well!' Rot said.

'What?' His father looked at him, surprised.

'Pyr8 and Gyr8 are very ill, Dad,' asserted Rot, 'and so are you and Mom. It's the only way to get those instruments back!'

'I don't get it…'

'How…?'

'I have a plan,' Rot said. 'This is what we're going to…'

Suddenly, he stopped talking, raising a tentacle to

his beak. Had he heard someone outside…listening? Soundlessly, Rot shuffled to the door, threw it open and yanked in…

'Tumboo!'

'Uh…hi, everyone…' said the turtle, embarrassed.

'What're you doing, snooping around?'

Tumboo looked defiant. 'I heard there was a new medicine… Gyr8 and Pyr8 got their appetite back!'

'Appetite ba… Ha ha ha!' Rot roared.

The octopus family grinned.

'It's all very well to laugh,' Tumboo pouted. 'You don't know what it feels like to have just two helpings of dessert!'

'Sorry,' Rot said, struggling to control his laughter. 'There's the medicine. On the table.'

Tumboo didn't need a second invitation. The featherweight turtle leapt onto the table, grabbed the vial and poured its contents down her throat.

'Ooeerrchch!' Tumboo squawked.

'Aarrgghhh!' Tumboo croaked.

'Grroogghh!' Tumboo choked.

Like a geyser, she spewed the liquid out of her mouth. 'That…that's awful!'

'I thought it was delicious!' said Gyr8.

'Yummy!' agreed Pyr8.

But to poor Tumboo, it tasted dreadful. The wonderful octopus medicine was no help at all! The woebegone turtle's appetite was still lost—and she was beginning to wonder if she would ever find it again.

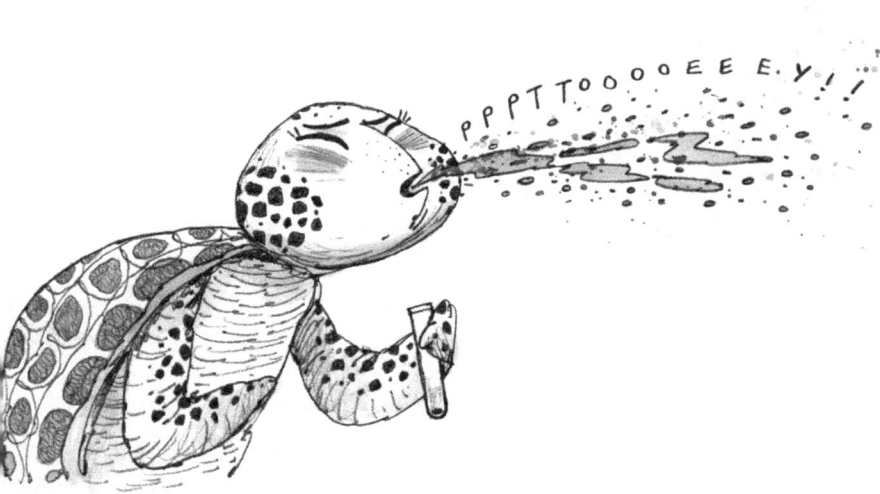

8

'They chose us?'

Po couldn't believe his ear-sac.

He'd known that all four members of Rot's family had fallen ill. He knew that the Octopus Selection Committee was to hold an emergency meeting to select replacements for the Oct-estra. In fact, Irrit, Po, Imit and Emul had applied for the suddenly vacant positions, but Po was sure they had no chance. So he was shocked when Irrit swam up with the news that they had indeed been selected.

'But…but…we're terrible!' Po exclaimed.

'Well…I wouldn't say "terrible"…' Irrit objected.

'We've no talent at all!' Po continued.

'That's not true!' Irrit argued. 'Ms Reson8 herself recommended us!' (Ms Reson8 was Sea World

School's music teacher.)

'But we can't play a note!' When Po started on the truth, he just couldn't stop. 'And anyway, how are we going to play when we've hidden the…'

Irrit clapped a tentacle onto Po's beak, cutting off the blabbering bard.

'Shut up and listen!' Irrit hissed into Po's ear-sac. 'We haven't hidden a thing! And if we do stumble across the instruments, purely by luck of course, we'll have saved the show! We'll be heroes!'

Po's eyes widened.

'And you know who loves heroes?' Irrit went on, cunning as ever. 'Females!'

Po's eyes grew dreamy. Carefully, Irrit unwound his tentacle from around the poet's beak.

'Female turtles?' Po asked hopefully.

'Particularly female turtles!'

Po grinned. 'You can count on me, Irrit.'

'Finding what's lost is not so tough,

Specially when you know where you've hidden the stuff!'

'Heh heh heh,' Irrit laughed nervously, feeling he had uncovered Po's beak too soon.

Anyway, this was their big chance. They would retrieve the instruments from Sesame and then… They would be the stars of the show, everyone would love them, they would finally show up Rot and Tumboo! For a moment, Irrit felt a twinge of concern about his group's talent. Could Po be right? Were they truly awful? But then Irrit put the niggle firmly out of his mind. They must be good. After all, Ms Reson8 had recommended them, hadn't she?

Po was completely right, of course. Irrit, Po, Imit and Emul had not a talented bone in their bodies. Why, then, had the Selection Committee chosen them for the Oct-estra? Three hours ago, Rot's parents had met Ms Reson8 secretly to discuss Rot's plan to recover the missing instruments. They said that they suspected Irrit and Po—they were all convinced that that pesky pair was behind the burglary. Rot's family was pretending to be ill so that new players could be appointed to the Oct-estra. Rot wanted Ms Reson8 to select Irrit and his friends—were that to happen, Rot was certain the instruments would reappear at once! Ms Reson8 had laughed and agreed. And shortly, Irrit and gang were selected for the Oct-estra.

Septopus

In the dead of the night, when no other water creature was around to point a fin at them, Irrit, Po, Imit and Emul slithered into Clam Cove.

'Open, Sesame,' Po whispered to the giant clam.

Sesame's huge mouth groaned open. There, right in the middle of the clam's fleshy mantle, lay a large, white blob—and nothing else!

'What the—?' reacted Irrit. 'Where are the instruments?'

'Uh…I think…' Po pointed a hesitant tentacle at the blob.

Irrit looked disgusted. 'You mean he's squirted his stomach juices all over them?'

'Heh heh…' Po tittered, apologetically. 'Luckily, we got here before he digested them, huh?'

Grossed out, the octopuses moved into Sesame's mouth and dug into the revolting blob, tugging at the instruments.

'Ick!' uttered Irrit.

'Yuck!' sputtered Imit.

'Stuck!' complained Emul, his tentacles caught in the gluey bog. 'What a mess!'

'Shh!' Po whispered. 'Don't hurt Sesame's feelings!'

Sesame's feelings! Ha! And what about their feelings, tramping in his gross goo? But no one voiced that thought. They weren't going to take a chance—not when that mammoth mouth could crash shut right on top of them!

Panting and straining, the gang finally got the instruments out of Sesame's sticky shells and piled them on the floor of the tank.

'Phew!' Irrit breathed. 'For a minute there, I thought we'd never get free. I wouldn't want to go through that again!'

SHRRRRSSSS!

A net hissed through the water, snagging Irrit, Imit and Emul!

Even as they struggled, the net rose out of the water and moved beyond the enclosing glass walls of Clam Cove into the adjacent viewing area. Po watched in horror as the net dumped the flailing octopuses into a container on top of a large trolley. A Sea World worker stood next to a machine, manipulating levers that controlled the menacing net. It rushed forward again, plunging into the water. Terrified, Po stumbled back. The net missed him, but scooped up the musical

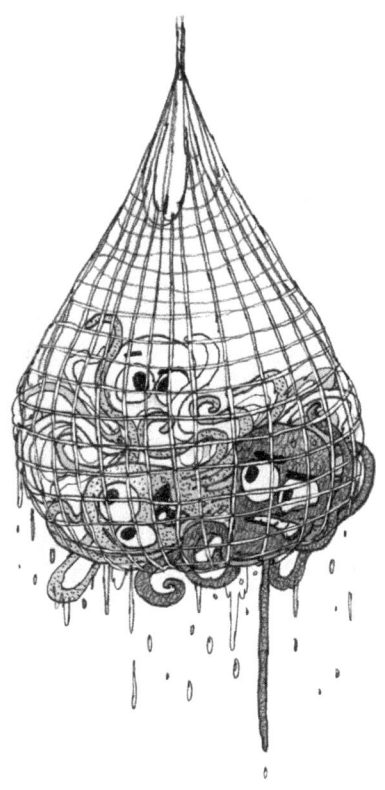

instruments and bore them away. Tipping the violins and cellos, trombones and trumpets into a second container, the net slithered into the tank once more, swooping down to grab the lone octopus remaining. Wide-eyed, petrified, Po saw it coming. Abruptly, he remembered his funnel, shot water through it and fled towards the pool exit. He was too late—the net was there already, blocking his getaway. It snaked forward, driving at Po like the maw of a hungry sea serpent from which there was no escaping. Desperate, Po skittered away, looking for a grill, a hatch, any opening in the smooth, uncaring walls of the enclosure. There was nothing.

But then, all at once, his terror-stricken mind came up with an idea: Sesame!

Po streaked towards the giant clam's mouth and crashed into the sticky mantle, the very place from which the octopuses had pulled out the instruments minutes ago. Dazed, Po turned around to look. The net was twisting, changing its course to make for the octopus sprawled in the clam's mouth.

'Zip the lip, Sesame!' Po screamed.

The enormous upper shell dropped. The Sea World worker tried to speed up the net, but he couldn't quite make it—the last thing Po saw was the worker's red-and-yellow shoe stamping in frustration as the shells crashed shut.

∞

Things hadn't worked out as Rot had anticipated. Despite Irrit's group being selected as replacements, there was no sign of the missing instruments. In fact, there was no sign of Irrit and his gang, either! Where could they be? When there were no answers all morning, the worried grown-ups decided to search every lair, den and cove in Sea World. Messages were sent out to all water creatures to immediately comb through their areas and report any sighting of the missing group. But when word came back, the story was the same: there was not the slightest trace of the absent octopuses.

There were three areas, though, that hadn't reported in: Whale Waters, Shark Shoals and Clam Cove. If the group had wandered into the first two areas then that was the last anyone was going to see of them—no one came back from the domains of the water giants! Clam Cove, however, needed to be investigated and the anxious parents of the lost lads accompanied by Mr Babbar, the sea lion (Sea World School's principal), made their way there. There was a reason, of course, that no information had come in from this area. There is no water creature as close-mouthed as a clam and when Mr Babbar and the others arrived at Clam Cove, they could see this for themselves. Every clam had its mouth shut tightly, shells sealed. Mr Babbar tried explaining to them that this was serious, that they were looking for lost youngsters, but the clams just lay there, silent, unmoving.

'It hopeless,' Mr Babbar sighed (in Fishy, which no one spoke well). 'They clammed up!'

'One minute, Mr Babbar,' said an octopus.

This was Po's mother and she knew that her son had a friend in Clam Cove. Unfortunately, she didn't know who it was, but she had to try.

'I, Po's mother,' she said to all the clams in Fishy. Her voice trembled as she continued, 'My son and friends gone, know not where. I know Po friend here. If you see him please help me. Please help friend.'

A tear slipped out of her eye, unnoticed in the water.

Suddenly, a loud groan rolled through the water. Startled, the water dwellers noticed that Sesame, the biggest clam of all, was opening his mouth. They looked at each other excitedly; was the giant going to say something?

'PTOOOIIIEEE!'

Sesame spat out a huge, white glob of goo straight at Mr Babbar!

Septopus

'Ugh!' Mr Babbar spluttered. The creature had spat on him! Never had he been so offended. 'I had it! Let get out of here!' He brushed off the blob and started to leave.

'Wait moment!'

Po's mother rushed forward to the blob and tore away at it. A shiny face emerged, eyes closed, unconscious.

'Po! My son!'

Awed, the water creatures turned and looked at Sesame.

A deep voice rumbled, 'Po...'

9

'He's still unconscious…' Dr Reena Renaldo muttered, worried.

Rot heard the words as 'Heesti llunconaee sciousaa', which made no sense whatsoever. But he knew what the Lab Lady was muttering about. Po lay unmoving in a water-filled container in Reena's Creature Clinic. Rot had watched as Reena tried everything to revive Po, even spooning the wonderful new octopus medicine into his beak, but the syrup had just dribbled out of his mouth. Rot knew what had to be done. The medicine had to be forced down Po's throat into his stomach. And there was just one way to do that!

'You want me to blow that awful-tasting medicine into *Po's mouth?*' Tumboo was outraged.

'It's our duty to help the sick,' Rot remarked, a pious expression on his face.

'Duty? Don't talk to me about duty!' Tumboo barked. 'If I never hear that word again, it'll be too soon!'

Rot hid a grin and sighed, shaking his head gloomily.

Tumboo looked at him and groaned. There was no way out. 'All right, all right, I'll do it,' she said, giving up.

Through a series of gestures, Rot tried to explain to Reena and Zubbu what they wanted to do.

'I think they're telling us to lift the sick octopus out of the water,' Reena guessed.

'But the turtle wantz to drink the medizine…' mumbled Zubbu, confused.

'No…' Reena understood what Rot was trying to convey. 'It seems the turtle's going to blow the medicine into the octopus. Isn't that clever?'

'H'aztonizhing!'

The scientists lifted Po out of the container. Holding her nose, Tumboo took a sip of the medicine. Then, hurriedly, she shut her eyes, pressed her lips against Po's slimy mouth and spurted the syrup down his throat. Po didn't stir. Much to her disgust, Tumboo had to repeat the process. And then do it again. The fourth time this happened, Po's eyes fluttered open and he saw…Tumboo, her eyes shut tightly, her lips glued on his! Po couldn't believe it! If this were a dream, he didn't want it to end! He slammed his eyes shut, pretending he was still knocked out. Unluckily for Po, Rot noticed his eyes' giveaway action.

'Ha ha ha!' Rot roared.

Startled, Tumboo jerked back, looked at Po and caught on.

'Blechchch!' she retched, scrubbing her mouth so fiercely it looked as if she'd rub her lips right off!

The scientists understood, too.

'He's awake,' said Reena, lowering Po into the water. She looked at Rot and Tumboo fondly. 'That was marvellous!'

'H'een-credi-bull!' Zubbu agreed.

Rot shuffled up to the side of the tank. He grinned at Po, who was still pretending, unmoving, eyes squeezed shut.

'It's no use, Po,' Rot chuckled. 'The jig's up!'

Septopus

Po stirred and pretended to awaken. 'Uhhh...I feel woozy... Maybe some more of that syrup...' He looked at Tumboo hopefully.

'Don't push your luck!' Tumboo snapped. 'And if you don't cough up answers right away, you slimy slug of spittle, I'll...I'll...'

She didn't know what she'd do, but she was sure it would be something terrible!

Po didn't have to be persuaded, though. A poem drifted into the batty bard's brain:

Oh, when she lovingly calls me
'Slimy slug of spittle',
It enchants me and enthrals me,
Oh, I just melt, little by little!

As far as the amorous octopus was concerned, anything Tumboo wanted, Tumboo could have! Almost before Rot asked him, Po poured out the entire story: the spiriting away of the musical instruments by Irrit and gang, concealing them inside Sesame, the nightmarish net attack, Irrit and the others being captured, Po's escape by hiding in the giant clam.

'And the net?' Rot questioned. 'Was there a human

controlling it?'

'Yeah...' Po hesitated, remembering. 'Yes, there was...'

A current of excitement ran through Rot. 'Did you get a look at his shoes?' he asked.

Shoes? thought Po. Were those the things humans wore on their feet? He had no idea what the net-controlling human had on. But he couldn't admit that. Tumboo was looking at him and this was his chance to score points with her, to be a hero. He had to come up with a description of those human feet-things.

'I remember!' he said, striking a noble pose, befitting a hero.

'Why's he swelling up like a backed-up blowfish?' Tumboo asked Rot.

Rot laughed. Po looked hurt and sagged back to his normal weedy self.

'The shoes?' Rot reminded him.

Grumpily, Po said, 'They were blue with metal thingamajigs on top!'

Which was a perfect description of the buckled shoes at which Po was looking, just behind Rot and Tumboo, on the feet of Dr Reena Renaldo!

Septopus

The news spread like an oil slick in the ocean. Very quickly, all the water creatures learnt what had happened to Irrit and his cousins. But the humans had no idea at all. Rot had tried very hard to explain matters to Reena, but the story of the net and the octo-napping was too complicated to be told through gestures. Rot, however, wasn't prepared to sit back and do nothing. Not for a moment did he believe Po—he knew that the sneaky songster had just described the Lab Lady's footwear (Rot was very observant and he had seen those shoes on Reena's feet umpteen times). So he decided to personally check out the crime scene.

With Tumboo in tow, Rot slipped into the viewing area adjacent to Clam Cove. All was quiet in the water-

filled tank beyond the glass wall. In any case, Rot knew that there would be nothing to discover in the water—it was the dry side that had to be investigated. Taking the magnifying glass attachment from Tumboo and snapping it onto his halfway limb, Rot inched over the floor. The tiles had been vacuum-cleaned and there was not even a speck of dust. There is one thing, though, that is immune to the tug of a vacuum cleaner. In a corner, clearly visible through his magnifier, were traces of tar—in the shape of a sneaker sole!

Rot smiled grimly. So it was the same human again, the one who had stepped onto the freshly tarred road: the man with red-and-yellow shoes!

༄

'There!'

'Where?' Rot swivelled the binoculars fastened to his halfway limb, looking in the direction indicated by Tumboo. They were again atop the tallest coconut tree in Sea World, trying to spot the man in red-and-yellow shoes. Tumboo pointed at a group of three men standing next to an impressive yacht docked at the Sea World pier. Rot recognized two of them, but the third wasn't familiar.

'The fat one?' he asked.

'Yeah,' Tumboo sighed. 'Doesn't he look like he has a healthy appetite?'

Rot shot a look at the turtle. Obviously, Tumboo had more important things on her mind than looking for a pair of shoes! Still, the fat man did look unusual. Rot noted the moustached, florid face, the shiny stones on the earlobes, then tilted his binoculars down to look at the man's feet. Unluckily, the man was standing on the yacht's gangway and the shoes were hidden.

'Thank you for the tour,' Jai Kalia said to the two Sea World employees. 'I'm sure you have everything in control.'

'Uh…' the Senior Super mumbled.

'Everything fipfape!' the Junior Super beamed, using a nautical term to impress the man who owned such a beautiful boat.

Kalia smiled and boarded his yacht.

'No,' Rot said. The fat man's shoes had become visible as he stepped onto the yacht's deck. 'They're brown and white. And anyway, he's not our man. He's too fat!'

'Healthy!' insisted Tumboo.

As Rot watched, the yacht moved away from the dock. The wind caught the sails, they filled and stretched, unfurling colours, revealing a design. There, woven across the vast sailcloth was:

10

'That octopus!'

'What?' asked Tumboo.

'The octopus on that boat's sail!' Rot exclaimed. 'It's the same one that the bad man's travelling machine stamped on my back!'

'So?'

'So there's a link between the man in red-and-yellow shoes and the fat man!' Rot noticed that the yacht was getting farther away from the dock. 'We've got to follow them!'

'Why?' Tumboo was busy tying more coconuts to the tree, saving them for the happier days when she could tuck into them again. She didn't see any reason to go running after a fat human who'd just remind her of her lost appetite.

'I think the fat man's behind it all!' Rot said. 'The missing instruments...'

Tumboo looked bored.

'Irrit being kidnapped...'

'Best thing anyone ever did!'

'Your appetite vanishing...'

'The bandit! The thief! The fat so-and-so! Let's get him, Rot! Uh...how?'

It was a good question. The yacht had pulled too far away to jump on board and swimming to it was out—Rot and Tumboo could no longer get into the water. Abruptly, the roar of an engine shattered the quiet of the seafront. Watersports are big in Goa and a speedboat whizzed by, trailing a hang-glider that was rising from the water.

'That kite-thing!' exclaimed Rot. 'Tumbs! Go for it!'

'What? That's nuts!'

'Just do it!'

Rot snapped a clamp onto his halfway limb and grabbed hold of Tumboo with another tentacle. As the glider rose to treetop level, the featherweight turtle shut her eyes and...

Septopus

'SUUUPERTURTLE!' yelled Tumboo to keep her nerve, and leapt!

For a moment, she did look like a superhero, flying through the air with Rot flapping from her shell like a cape. They streaked through the air, almost knocking the beak off a passing gull that got the shock of its life! Eleven-and-a-half legs and a shell! What sort of bird was that?! For a novice flyer, though, Tumboo had timed her leap perfectly. They reached the rising glider, Rot snapped his halfway limb forward and the clamp hooked neatly onto an aluminium strut. Rot weighed very little and Tumboo in her present condition weighed nothing at all. The hanging human didn't even notice that there were a couple of extra passengers on his glider. It rose smoothly, high into the air until the sea spread out below them like a vast blue sky turned upside down.

'Oh, shellfish!' gasped Tumboo, dangling from Rot's tentacle. Turtles were definitely not meant to fly!

There was no denying, though, that the view was breathtaking. Hanging from the glider, high in the sky, Rot and Tumboo could see all the beauty of Goa: the ink-blue sea rolling in, breaking into foaming white

waves as it ran onto the soft sand of the beaches, the ring of graceful palm trees nodding in the breeze, dozens of boats of every kind, skipping over the waves, their colours standing out against the sea like petals strewn in ponds after rain.

'There she goes!' shouted Rot, pointing at a tall sail, the octopus painted on it very visible, stretching its tentacles into the wind.

'Are we following it?'

'Not likely, Tumbs...'

And Rot was proven right immediately. The boat to which their glider was attached started turning away.

'I need the umbrella,' Rot said, coiling another tentacle around the glider strut and unhooking the clamp.

Tumboo reached into her shell and pulled out a 'U' pouch. Rot attached it to his halfway limb and whipped it forward. Out popped an umbrella!

'Got it in one go, again!' Rot grinned. 'Not eating really works for you!'

Tumboo looked glum. 'What're you going to do with that?' she asked, indicating the umbrella.

'It's Superturtle time again!' Rot said, unfolding the umbrella.

Instantly, the wind filled the umbrella canopy and snatched them off the glider. The two water dwellers floated away, a hundred feet above the sea.

'Yaaahhhhh!' cried Tumboo, desperately hanging on to Rot's tentacle, goggling at the waves, way, way, WAY down there!

Down there was the yacht with the octopus sail and inside the yacht's plush cabin was the fat man. Jai Kalia was in a great mood. He had enjoyed watching the Senior Supervisor squirm. The Sea World official had anxiously tried to hide the disappearance of the Oct-estra from Kalia, fearing that the sponsor would pull his money out. Little did he know that Kalia himself had purloined the instruments and abducted the octopuses!

And here they all were, three terrified octopuses and sixteen specially designed underwater musical instruments—in a glass tank in the yacht's cabin, right in front of Kalia.

'You should have been there, Gomes!' Kalia laughed. 'That twerp tied himself into knots pretending that all was well!'

Gomes (for that was the name of the man in red-and-yellow shoes) grinned.

'And you know what his assistant said?' Kalia continued. '"Everything fipfape"! Fipfape! Ha ha ha ha!'

ೞ

Kalia didn't know it, but everything wasn't shipshape for him, either. Fifty feet above, descending towards the yacht, was a most unlikely parachute.

As the umbrella floated down, its canopy snagged on the masthead and it stopped with a jerk. The hanging octopus and turtle slammed into the yacht's mainsail.

'Yaaaaaaaahhhhhhhhhh-OOF!' went Tumboo.

As superhero arrivals go, it wasn't the most inspiring. Very few superheroes are left dangling on top of a mast when they fly in to save the day.

'What do we do now?' demanded Tumboo, her head spinning at the dizzying distance between the masthead and the deck below.

'We shin down this,' Rot pointed a tentacle at the

tall mast. 'Just think of it as a coconut tree without coconuts!'

'The only octopus orchestra in the world and now it belongs to me!' Kalia gloated in his cabin. He jabbed a conductor's baton towards the octopuses in the tank. 'Let's see if you're as good as they say,' he grinned. 'Play!'

Irrit8, Imit8 and Emul8 looked at the fat man. They thought him terrifying! And when a scary human jabs a stick, obviously wanting one to play, one doesn't argue.

Septopus

Irrit picked up four instruments and started in on them.

So did Imit, imitating Irrit.

So did Emul, emulating Imit.

The instruments were connected to an amplifier and powerful speakers. The octopuses' music streamed out, a carefully selected mix of:

1. nails scraping a blackboard;
2. the foghorn of a barge;
3. garbage cans clanging; and
4. a cat mewling in those clanging cans.

'Ow!' yelled Kalia, staggering, clapping his hands over his diamond-studded ears.

Gomes stumbled back against the wall, right next to the amplifier. Desperately, he hit the power button.

A sudden silence descended. Realizing that the sound had ceased, the octopuses stopped playing and grinned at each other. That was terrific! No wonder Ms Reson8 had recommended them!

Kalia shook his head, his ears numb. He looked shattered.

'W…what was that?' he squeaked.

'M...maybe dey're tuning de instruments...' gasped Gomes.

'Could be...' Kalia was still shaken. 'Let's try again...'

Hesitantly, Gomes pushed the power button. Nervously, Kalia raised his baton. Then closing his eyes, he pointed the stick at Irrit and Co.

11

Rot and Tumboo had just touched down on deck when the horrendous noise started again. There were three layers of noise-cancelling carbon fibre between the cabin and deck, but the nerve-grating sound was unmistakable.

'Yep,' nodded Rot. 'That's Irrit! We've found them!'

'Can't we lose them again?' said Tumboo, clapping her flippers over her ears.

In the cabin, Gomes frantically hit the power button again, but it was stuck! There was nothing to protect the conspirators from Irrit's musical genius. The sound roared and banged and crashed around the cabin. Kalia reeled, feeling as if the yacht was pitching and rolling, caught in angry seas. Of course, the only seas involved were Irrit's screeching high Cs, but that made no difference to Kalia. His head whirled, his senses swirled; was he hallucinating? Did he have octopuses on the brain or was that indeed an octopus he could see at the porthole, peering into the cabin?

On the deck outside, at the guardrail, stood a tubby turtle, carefully holding a fishhook. A nylon line from the fishhook led down the hull of the yacht all the way to a porthole, where it met up with a fishing rod, firmly attached to Rot's halfway limb. Hanging from the rod and line, Rot looked through the porthole into the cabin and chuckled.

Obviously, the fat man and the man in red-and-yellow shoes were not enjoying Irrit and Co.'s music.

'Tumboo's got to see this!'

Septopus

Of course, it couldn't be an octopus outside the porthole! Kalia shut his eyes and shook his head. The spinning seemed to slow down. He opened his eyes again, looked at the porthole, and saw...

'A turtle!'

Outside, the positions were reversed. Rot sat on the deck, fishing rod on his halfway limb, holding the featherweight Tumboo level with the porthole at the end of the fishing line. Tumboo guffawed—Rot was right; the staggering scoundrels were a scream!

Kalia turned to Gomes. 'Am I seeing things?' he shouted above the mind-deadening din. 'Is that a turtle or octopus?'

'Where?'

'There!' hollered Kalia, turning towards the porthole—it was empty! Kalia goggled in disbelief. 'The noise! It's driving me crazy! Do something!'

'De mains!' yelled Gomes. 'We gotta switch off de power!'

He yanked the cabin door open and tottered out, heading for the engine room where the mains were located. Unfortunately, he failed to spot an almost invisible fishing line stretched across the deck. Gomes tripped on the line, tumbled over the guardrail and pitched headfirst into the limpid Goa sea!

'Human overboard!' chorused Rot and Tumboo, slapping tentacle and flipper together in a 'high-one'.

'Help!' spluttered the human, floundering in the waves.

Rot and Tumboo knew that humans were pretty helpless creatures, prone to drowning easily. Rot swung the fishing rod; the line flew over the water and the hook snagged a red-and-yellow shoe.

'I've got a bite,' Rot grinned. 'Reel him in?'

'Nah,' Tumboo chortled. 'Keep him there awhile. Those socks really need a wash!'

'What's that clown doing?' Kalia muttered, jabbing again and again at the stuck power button in the cabin. 'Why hasn't he switched off the mains?'

Irrit and gang were blasting away and Kalia was being reduced to a quivering mass of jelly. He tried thrusting and waving his baton threateningly at the octopuses.

'Check it out!' Irrit said, indicating the fat human's lively movements. 'We're really rocking him!'

Appreciation from fans energizes performers and

Septopus

the octopuses poured even more of their 'talent' into their playing.

'I can't take it!' Kalia howled.

Violently, he pulled open the cabin door and reeled out.

'Help!'

Was that a voice he heard? Kalia turned to look and his jaw dropped. Forty feet adrift of the yacht was his assistant, Gomes, struggling in the sea. He was being pulled along by a line, a fishing line that led to a fishing rod held by an…octopus!

Kalia's head whirled. He closed his eyes, and then reluctantly opened them again. They were still there: Gomes in the sea, the fishing line, the rod, but it was now held by a...turtle! An unusually plump turtle standing on its hind feet, leaning casually against the guardrail! Kalia clutched his head. Was he going mad? He rushed to the bridge of the yacht and snatched open the door. Startled, the pilot turned from the ship's wheel. Jai Kalia, the owner of the yacht, the big boss himself, stood in the doorway, wild-eyed, looking like a madman! But the pilot wasn't paid to comment on the boss' looks. He quickly straightened and saluted.

'Tell me,' Kalia said to the pilot in a hoarse, strained voice, 'what do you see starboard?'

Puzzled, the pilot looked through the windows of the bridge and he goggled in astonishment.

'It's Gomes, sir! He's fallen into the sea!'

'Yes, yes,' Kalia said, seeming reluctant to look himself, 'but do you see the fishing line he's snagged on?'

'Yes, sir! It's attached to a fishing rod!'

'And the turtle holding the rod? Do you see the turtle?'

'Turtle, sir?'

Kalia spun around and groaned. He definitely must be going mad! There *was* a rod, but it was lodged firmly in the guardrail, all by itself. Where a fat turtle had stood, there was only thin air!

12

With tentacles and flippers covering ear-sac and ears, Rot and Tumboo warily entered the yacht's cabin. The music from hell exploded in their faces, bursting past their feeble ear protection.

'Stop playing, Irrit!' Rot yelled.

But even if he could have heard, Irrit was in no mood to listen. Here was a chance to hit back at Rot and Tumboo, his hated rivals. He'd show them what real music was! He let fly with another cacophonic chord.

'Every turtle for herself!' Tumboo muttered and disappeared into her shell like a jack-in-the-box in reverse.

'This is no time to retreat into your shell!' scolded

Rot. 'I need a screwdriver!'

A flipper popped out, holding an 'S' pouch. Fixing it to his halfway limb, Rot snapped it forward.

'Right again!' Rot grinned. 'I really don't know why you want your appetite back!'

A hollow groan sounded from somewhere within the shell.

Rot scurried to the amplifier. Earlier, through the porthole, he had seen the humans jabbing the little round thing on the box, and he knew where the problem lay. He inserted the screwdriver into the tiny crevice next to the power button and jiggled it. There was a sudden flash and two things happened: the stuck button popped out, and Rot was hurled away from the amplifier. The maddening music stopped.

'Hey!' Tumboo emerged from her shell. 'The racket's ended! That's terrific, Rot! Whatever you did—it worked!'

But Rot was just lying there. Not moving.

'Rot? Rot!' Tumboo hurried over. 'Rot, what's wrong? Are you okay?'

Rot's eyes opened. 'I…I'm all right, Tumbs…I think…'

But he wasn't. He tingled all over as if the electric charge that had flung him across the room was still running through his body.

'Music...' he mumbled. 'I need a mu...music player...'

'Yeah, sure,' Tumboo replied, reaching into her shell. 'But are you... I mean, you're all right, aren't you? You don't sound it...'

Rot was finding it difficult to breathe. And he knew the feeling. He had experienced it earlier, all his life, before he had eaten the mixed-up food in the lab. It was the feeling an octopus has when he's been out of the water too long.

'Q...quick...' Rot wheezed.

Hurriedly, the turtle handed over a pouch marked 'M'. Rot snapped it on, flipped it forward and smiled when a music player emerged, attached to his limb.

'Still d...doing great, Tumbs! Now get me into the tank...fast!'

'Into the...in the water?' Tumboo was aghast. 'But you'll drown!'

'Don't w...worry...' Rot panted. 'Just d...do it!'

Irrit, Imit and Emul were glaring at Rot and

Tumboo—if looks could kill, Rot and Tumboo would have been soup! How dare they switch off the music just when Irrit and gang were hitting those never-heard-before notes!

Rot and Tumboo ignored them, of course. Tumboo hoisted Rot, swiftly carried him to the tank, leapt up to the rim and gently lowered Rot into the water.

Rot sank to the bottom of the tank. He took a deep breath. And then another. Sweet water flowed through his gills, oxygen coursed through his body; Rot felt himself come alive. He flexed his tentacles and grinned—this was more like it! The effect of the food mixture was gone: the electric shock had neutralized it. He was back where he belonged.

Quickly, Rot glided to the glass wall of the tank. Tumboo stood on the other side, anxiously peering in. She grinned delightedly when Rot swam up and flipper and tentacle slapped the glass wall together (though on opposite sides) in the happiest 'high-one' ever!

Rot turned to face Irrit and his cronies, the missing instruments all around them.

'So we've found them, Tumbs!' Rot said. 'The plunder *and* the plunderers!'

Tumboo fixed an accusing eye on the trio. 'What have you got to say for yourselves, you moronic mounds of mucus?'

There really wasn't very much to say; Irrit and gang had been caught red-tentacled! And anyway, Irrit's bravado was on display only when Rot was nowhere around. He had seen Rot in action too often to act the big fish in his presence.

'So what do we do now?' muttered Irrit, sullen as ever.

'You do as I say,' Rot said.

'You do as Rot says!' Tumboo repeated, a no-nonsense note in her voice.

'Pick up those instruments,' said Rot.

'Pick up those instruments!' ordered Tumboo.

'And play!'

'And play! Whaaattt?' Tumboo looked at Rot in shock.

Irrit, Imit and Emul grinned. Playing their 'music' was just what they wanted to do. Maybe Rot wasn't so bad, after all!

'You can't be serious, Rot!' Tumboo protested. 'Their music—it's torture! It's cruelty!'

'Hey!' Irrit objected.

'It's…it's way beyond the call of duty!'

'I'll get you a medal, Tumbs!' grinned Rot. 'Just hit the button on that box when I tell you. And don't worry…I have a plan!'

∽

Kalia panted. The pilot wheezed. Gomes gasped. They lay on the deck, trying to recover their breath, having strained every limb and sinew in dragging Gomes out of the water.

'Y…you clumsy oaf!' Kalia spluttered. 'Falling into the water like a l…landlubber!'

'Wasn't m…my fault, b…boss!' Gomes muttered. 'C…couldn't do nutting… I was tri…'

'Shaddup!' Kalia barked.

Gomes shut up. The boss wasn't listening to him. He had his head cocked, hearing something else, listening to…

'That music!' Kalia breathed.

Borne on the soft wind was music, wonderful music, notes as pure as pearls, chords as clear as coral…

'It's Mozart!' Kalia exclaimed. 'The octopuses are playing Mozart!'

The cabin door burst open. Moving astonishingly quickly for a man of his bulk, Kalia charged in. Following on his heels were Gomes and the pilot. A steward and an engineer peered in from the doorway. None of them had believed their ears. But they had to believe their eyes! Right in front of them, in the glass-walled tank were three…no, *four* octopuses, though only three were playing. Playing marvellous, virtuoso music!

'I knew it!' Kalia gloated. 'They were simply warming up earlier! Just listen to them!'

Kalia closed his eyes, dreamily listening to the music. Mozart's *Serenade No. 13*—the playing almost on the level of the orchestra in Berlin conducted by Zubair Midha himself. Kalia remembered the cello strain in the next movement—Midha's own idea; it had given Kalia the chills. Ah, there it was, the octopuses had played it exactly.

The octopuses had played it exactly??

How had they done that? Music can't be replicated exactly—there's always some difference in the playing.

Kalia's eyes snapped open. And the first thing he saw was a…turtle! The tubby turtle! Standing next to the amplifier, waving its flippers in time with the music! The turtle noticed him staring and gestured towards the tank. Kalia turned to look. What was it the turtle wanted him to see? The three octopuses were busy playing their instruments, but the fourth caught Kalia's attention. It wasn't playing music…or was it? This octopus wasn't holding a musical instrument, but what was that little, flat cube that seemed fastened to an underdeveloped tentacle? Was it…a music player? It was—and the lead from the amplifier was plugged not into the instruments but *into the little cube*! The fourth octopus raised the cube and waved it in Kalia's direction, as if saying, 'Look what I've got, a music player!'

Kalia could almost see the bulb that lit up inside his head!

'It's a hoax!' he shouted, laughing. 'The famous Sea World Oct-estra—it's just a sneaky little trick!'

'T…trick, boss?'

Kalia pointed. 'The music player, Gomes! That's the thing playing Mozart! The octopuses are simply banging away at the instruments, any which way! That's all they've been trained to do! It's a cheap circus act!' Kalia looked at the pilot. 'Turn this yacht around. We're going back to Sea World!'

The pilot saluted and left.

'B…but, boss,' Gomes stammered, 'we got de octopuses and instruments on board. What if someone…'

'Here's our story, Gomes,' Kalia interrupted. 'We intercepted a boat trying to smuggle the octopuses out of Goa and managed to get the creatures and instruments back after a titanic struggle! We return the Oct-estra to Sea World so that the show can go on. We're heroes, Gomes!' Kalia laughed and laughed.

It didn't make any sense. Why did the boss want the show to go on after all their efforts to sabotage it? Gomes was baffled. But Rot wasn't! He didn't understand the fat man's words, but judging from his excitement and laughter on discovering the music player, Rot knew what the fat man was plotting. Rot could feel the yacht turn around. They were heading back to Sea World. The fat man was going to hand them back to the Sea World authorities, but he didn't intend to bring up the matter of the music player just then. No, he was going to wait for the right moment. The fat man had a plan. Which fitted right in with Rot's plan! Rot grinned and winked at Tumboo who winked right back, happy that Rot's plan was working. Now, if only getting her appetite back was a part of that plan!

13

'And now, ladies and gentlemen, girls and boys,' boomed the announcer's voice, 'the moment we've all been waiting for! Sea World is proud to present the world-famous…OCTESTRA!'

Zubair Midha led the thunderous applause. Two days had flashed past and it was showtime! The place was packed—there were more than five thousand people watching the show live and hundreds of thousands more watching on TV screens all over the world. But how had five thousand people and dozens of TV cameras squeezed into the tiny Octestra chamber? Well, they hadn't! Much to the delight of the Senior Supervisor, the sponsor, Mr Jai Kalia, had personally paid for the construction of a new, glass-walled Oct-estra chamber right in front of Sea World's vast spectator galleries.

'My idea,' said the Junior Super proudly to a TV interviewer. 'Built on the feel'f platform.'

'Feelf?'

From an outcrop in the central pool, Rot and Tumboo watched the fat man. They knew why the new Oct-estra chamber had been built there. The fat man wanted everyone to see what he was about to show them. He was sitting confidently in the front row, next to the man everybody was making a fuss over.

'I'm really looking forward to this,' said Zubair Midha. 'I hear the octopuses play Mozart brilliantly!'

'I hope they play *Serenade No. 13*,' Kalia replied, smiling. 'There's a cello strain I'd like you to hear.'

A spotlight hit the Oct-estra chamber. Within its transparent walls Delic8, Clarin8, Gyr8 and Pyr8 floated in the water, their specially designed instruments poised. Ms Birdy walked down a narrow platform extending into the pool, bowed nervously to the audience and positioned herself in front of the octopuses.

'Ready, dikra?'

Septopus

Ms Birdy waved her baton and the Oct-estra launched into the piece: Mozart's *Serenade No. 13*!

The music washed over the enraptured audience. Zubair Midha listened, enthralled. Kalia watched him. The cello strain was just coming up; he wondered whether Midha would recognize it as his own immediately. Any moment now! Just then, a TV camera moved in to capture the reactions of the renowned conductor and the chief sponsor. Kalia promptly turned his head sideways to give the camera the benefit of his right profile (which he thought looked more aristocratic).

A beat, and then the camera pulled away. Kalia turned his attention to the music, but the moment had

passed. He was annoyed—the camera had distracted him and he had missed the cello. It didn't matter, though. He knew what he knew!

With a flourish, the Oct-estra reached the end of the piece.

'Bravo!' Zubair Midha shouted, clapping enthusiastically. 'Bravo!'

'Encore! Encore!' screamed the five thousand spectators.

'"Anchor" again!' Irrit spat, jealously watching the Oct-estra basking in audience applause. 'I'd like to tie an anchor on them and sink them!' He still couldn't understand why his gang and he had been dumped after their amazing playing.

But no one was paying any attention to an envious octopus in a dark corner of the pool. All eyes were on the front row where something unusual seemed to be happening.

'It's a recording!' Kalia said loudly, pretending to be taken aback. 'The octopuses have just played back your Berlin performance!' he said to Zubair Midha. 'The cello playing in the second movement is exactly the same!'

Septopus

'Not at all!' the conductor replied, concluding that the sponsor had no clue about music. 'It was quite different. And very good, indeed!'

This time Kalia didn't have to act taken aback—he was! He recovered quickly, however. Obviously, the octopuses had used another recording of *Serenade No. 13*.

'Be that as it may,' said Kalia, voice rising, 'I have just received some very disturbing information about this so-called Oct-estra!'

The reaction was instantaneous. Like vultures, the reporters swooped on Kalia, demanding details. This was precisely what Kalia wanted: a media circus! He would expose the hoax, humiliate the organizers in full view of thousands of people. The scandal would shut down the Oct-estra and with their most popular show revealed as a fraud, Sea World would close for good! Kalia and his partners would move in; within months they would build a beachfront hotel right where Sea World had stood. Kalia would make millions!

'You say this is a hoax, Mr Kalia! What evidence do you have?' a reporter demanded.

'What's the source of your information?'

'Can you prove it?'

Kalia held up his hand. The hubbub died down.

'You've already got the proof—on camera!' Kalia declared. He pointed at Ms Birdy. 'The conductor! She was waving her baton, but the music had as much connection with her conducting as the earth has with the moon!'

'The earth *is* connected to the moon!' pointed out a reporter.

'Directly connected!'

'Through gravity!'

'So you mean the music was directly connected to her conducting?'

'There's no connection!' Kalia screeched. He couldn't understand why people always got confused. 'The octopuses weren't following her at all! That proves that they weren't really playing!'

'That's not true, dikra!'

Everyone swung around. Ms Birdy trembled as thousands of eyes and dozens of cameras focused on her.

'Sorry for doing ting-ting in the middle,' she squeaked.

'You mean they *were* following your directions?' a reporter asked.

'No, they weren't,' Ms Birdy admitted.

'See?' Kalia gloated. 'That proves it!'

'They weren't following my directions,' Ms Birdy continued, 'because they don't need me. The octopuses know much more about music than me!'

Uproar followed this statement. Reporters yelled questions at Kalia and Ms Birdy, but nothing could be heard in the din. And right into the middle of this hullaballoo strolled a most unlikely pair: a turtle that walked upright and an octopus with seven-and-a-half tentacles. The sight was odd enough to silence even the tough, seen-it-all journalists. Kalia goggled. That octopus again! And the fat turtle! What were they up to now? Rot and Tumboo stopped in front of Zubair Midha.

'The p…pouch, Tumbs,' Rot panted, his oxygen level getting low.

Tumboo reached into her shell and pulled out a pouch marked 'B'. Rot attached it to his halfway limb and snapped it forward. Out sprang: a conductor's baton! The crowd murmured. Even Kalia and Zubair

Midha looked at Rot in surprise. Rot pointed at the maestro, gestured at the Oct-estra and waved the baton.

The humans looked confused, not understanding. This wasn't good. Rot was out in the open air and he knew he had very little time. He repeated his actions, waving the baton energetically.

'Isn't he clever?'

All eyes swivelled in the direction of the voice.

Dr Reena Renaldo stepped forward. 'He's asking *you* to conduct the Oct-estra, Mr Midha. If *you're*

convinced the octopuses play music, that's proof enough for anyone!'

'She's right!'

'That would prove it!'

'What an idea!'

'Brilliant!'

'He's just the cleverest creature I've ever seen!' Reena said, smiling fondly at Rot.

14

It was the day after the concert and every face at Sea World was locked into one huge grin! The show was a roaring hit! Zubair Midha's opinion was loud and clear.

'They're absolutely brilliant!' the maestro had said. 'They took a few moments to get the hang of it, which proves that they were actually playing! And then they played flawlessly. The octopuses are the most talented musicians I have ever worked with!'

The audience had erupted and given the Oct-estra a standing ovation. The only person not standing was Jai Kalia—he was too busy looking for his jaw, which seemed to have dropped to his feet! The media, of course, was over the moon:

'IT'S TRUE! THE OCTOPUSES ARE

GENIUSES!' screamed a headline.

'TENTACULAR TRIUMPH!'

'MAESTRO MIDHA MESMERIZED!'

'ZHEY ARE AMAZING, ZAYZ ZUBAIR!'

(The last headline perhaps had something to do with the reporter having interviewed Zubbu.)

But the story of the incredible octopuses was not the only one grabbing headlines. The media was agog with the news that the Octopus Group had collapsed! Following the Oct-estra's triumph, Jai Kalia's partners had pulled out of his schemes. Kalia had tried to use their money, promising them a fortune once he took over Sea World, and the partners claimed he had cheated them. The police were looking into it and it was likely Kalia would be arrested.

'The octopus!' Kalia snapped at an enquiring reporter. 'It's all his fault!'

Since Kalia was known as The Octopus, the paper promptly reported that Kalia had confessed!

The clamour, of course, made not the slightest difference to the water creatures. For a few hours after their spectacular success, Rot and his family had been lionized by the humans at Sea World (the sea lions were a little confused about that), but things had settled down and were now back to normal. Or almost normal.

'It's all very well to celebrate,' grumbled Tumboo to Rot. 'The humans have been giving everyone the choicest tidbits, but no one thinks of me!'

Rot, who had surfaced to sympathize with his friend, rolled his eyes. However, he was careful not to say anything. Tumboo was pretty upset, as it was.

'Except Mom, of course,' continued the aggrieved turtle. 'She saved some papaya for me. And you know what? I had to stop at two! Can you believe that? Just two papaYOW!'

This wasn't a new fruit. The 'yow' was because Clumsy Claude had stepped on Tumboo's tail. The attendant was busy dismantling the lights strung up for the previous night's event and, as usual, had failed to notice the turtle. Someone else, though, had eyes only for Tumboo. Po lurked in a pool corner, jealously watching Tumboo talking to Rot. When would that gorgeous creature confide in him instead? thought Po. Why was it that poets always had a hard time with love?

'It's unfair!' lamented Tumboo.

Of course, she was thinking about papaya, not Po, as she flounced away. Unluckily, she didn't notice that Claude, that incredibly inattentive attendant, had carelessly left an exposed electrical wire in the grass. Tumboo stepped on it. There was a flash and the turtle shot like a fat cannonball back into the pool!

Po had no idea what hit him. Suddenly, there was this huge, green thing hurtling towards him. It crashed into him and he sank to the bottom of the pool.

'Tumboo! Tumbs!' Rot shouted, streaking to the spot where Tumboo had splashed down. He found his friend lying on the floor of the pool, dazed.

'Tumbs, are you hurt?'

'I...'

Tumboo was tingling all over. Something was definitely wrong. Or perhaps right?

'Are you all right, Tumbs? How do you feel?'

Tumboo looked at Rot in wonder. 'I feel...hungry!'

'Hungry?'

But Tumboo was already on the move, barrelling towards the surface.

'Tumbs! Where are you going?'

'The coconuts I saved!' Tumboo shouted as she swam. 'I'm going to eat them all! Finally!'

Rot looked at his fast-retreating friend for a moment, and then burst out laughing.

'She's killed him!'

Rot stopped laughing. He turned and saw Irrit next to the unconscious Po, staring at Rot accusingly.

'Don't be silly!' Rot said. 'We've done this before! All he needs is some oxygen. Tumboo! Tumbs!'

But the turtle was nowhere to be seen. This could get serious.

'What's the matter?'

Rot and Irrit spun around. Ms Reson8, the music teacher, swam up.

'It's Po8, ma'am,' Rot said.

'He's dead!' Irrit snarled.

'Nonsense!' said Ms Reson8. 'Let me see.' She examined the senseless songster. 'Nothing that a little oxygen wouldn't set right!'

And with that, she placed her beak on Po's gills. In-and-out she blew, in-and-out, and Po's eyes fluttered open.

'Aaahhh,' he sighed. 'That feels so good. Don't stop!'

Septopus

'There you go,' Ms Reson8 said briskly. 'Now don't squirt ink for a few hours and you'll be as good as new!'

She swam away.

'Was that...was that...Ms Reson8?' asked Po, a dreamy look in his eyes.

'Y...e...es,' said Irrit.

Po rose and glided off after Ms Reson8.

'Po! Where are you going?' called Irrit.

But Po didn't bother to answer. A snatch of song floated back:

'Oh, she's the one for me!
Yes, she's the one for me!'

'Not again!' groaned Irrit, slapping his head with a tentacle. He swam off after his fickle friend.

Rot laughed. So, things were back to normal. Well, almost normal.

The calm of the water was shattered by a huge splash.

'Rot! Rot!' Tumboo swam down like a panic-stricken tub.

'What is it, Tumbs? What's happened?'

'The coconuts!' Tumboo panted. 'They're still at

the top of the tree! I forgot I tied them there!'

'So? Just climb up and get them!'

'I can't!' wailed Tumboo. 'I'm too heavy! The effect of that foodamajig's gone!'

'Well, don't jump out of your shell,' Rot said, trying to calm her. 'We'll get them down.'

They rose to the surface and saw the coconut tree swaying gently in the breeze, all those luscious coconuts at the very top.

'All we need is a slingshot!' Rot said.

A smile spread across the turtle's face. 'Of course! Why didn't I think of that? One slingshot coming up!'

She slipped a confident flipper into her shell and pulled out a pouch marked 'S'. Rot snapped it onto his halfway limb and flicked it forward. Out popped: a sandwich!

'Oops!' said Tumboo.

Rot hid a smile. 'Try again,' he suggested.

Tumboo reached in.

A sausage.

Followed by:

~ sugar cubes

Septopus

- sultanas
- sardines
- samosas

'A slingshot, Tumbs,' Rot said, patiently.

'I've positively got it this time!' Tumboo said, yanking out another 'S' pouch. 'I can feel the strings!'

Rot snapped it forward.

Spaghetti.

'Oops!'

Rot laughed. Yes, things were definitely back to normal. At last.

Printed in the USA
CPSIA information can be obtained
at www.ICGtesting.com
CBHW021203150824
13133CB00012B/293